Sourdough
for All

gestalten

Kenny Jakobsson

Contents

Recipes

Better baking

MASTODON
LEVIATHAN
SURDEGSGOTT

Bread & me

I remember when I baked my very first sourdough bread. Well, my first edible sourdough bread, I should add. I'd tried countless times before, but they'd come out more like rock-hard frisbees than bread. My father-in-law (to be, at that time) turned up at our new apartment for an unexpected visit. I hadn't met him many times at that point, so I was trying to play my cards right.

My finished bread was cooling on a rack, just as it should. It was a big and handsome loaf, and smelled amazing, but I was still nervous about slicing it open, as its predecessors had all been almost inedible. And then my father-in-law walked into the kitchen and said something along the lines of:

"What's that lovely smell? Have you been baking?"

"Yes, well, kind of…" I mumbled, and thought: Dammit!

"I'm trying to bake sourdough bread," I finally answered. "Do you… want to try?"

"Yes, please!" He said.

I reluctantly cut a slice, and to my surprise it looked pretty good! I was delighted and grabbed the butter from the refrigerator, and we each started to make a sandwich. The bread was delicious and we stood there and chatted a while. I don't really remember what we spoke about, because all I could really think about was my bread. That's probably what he was thinking about, too. Probably about how he'd struck it lucky with a son-in-law who could bake such good bread.

My interest in bread began when I lived in Linnéstan in Gothenburg. Every weekend I'd go and buy a loaf at the sourdough bakery *Alvar & Ivar.* I'd never eaten bread like that before. Real bread. It was inconceivable to me that bread could taste that good. It didn't even taste like "bread," or at least not like the bread I'd been used to. This was something else!

Today, I can honestly say that baking sourdough bread is one of the most fun things I've learned as an adult. I love baking bread. I don't really know what it is, but it feels incredibly satisfying, almost meditative. Every bread is a surprise and no two are alike. By adjusting the type of flour and the amount of water, it's possible to create an almost infinite number of combinations and flavors. And then there's the reward—taking the baked loaf out of the oven. The aroma that wafts around the kitchen. The anticipation before cutting the bread—taking a look, taking a sniff, before finally spreading on a thick layer of butter and sinking your teeth into it. It's a tough one to beat.

I remember how deeply I fell in love with baking my own bread, weekend after weekend. I became engrossed in understanding how it worked as I learned more and more. I was so proud of my delicious creations. There was that strange feeling of giving away a loaf of bread when the recipient struggled to understand that I'd made something so pretty and delicious all by myself. I was like a five-year-old learning to tie their shoes, or whatever you do at that age. I was so proud! It may sound trivial—we're talking about baking bread after all—but I think there's something more to it. It's about understanding that good food not only takes time, but it also must be given that time if it's to be good.

For me, baking sourdough bread is about creating something from scratch. It's about slowly processing a few ingredients to get a wonderful result, made by you, with your own hands. That's powerful. If I were to give one piece of advice to everyone I know—and also those I don't know—it would be to learn to bake sourdough bread. You won't regret it.

If I can, so can you

When I started baking, I was utterly convinced that baking sourdough bread was one big scam. Read for yourself: Just mix together flour and water and let it stand. Then, in some magical way, this wizard known as sourdough will leaven the bread and make it taste delicious. I thought it sounded implausible, and my pathetic attempts to make well-risen sourdough bread only made matters worse. I thought everyone secretly added store-bought yeast. I was convinced that baking sourdough bread simply didn't work and that everyone was lying... Or that maybe there were just a handful of sourdough wizards in the world who had mastered the magic, and that the rest of us mortals simply weren't worthy. I now know better. Baking sourdough bread is very logical and actually just as easy as baking with the yeast you can buy at the store.

For the uninitiated, sourdough can be a difficult concept to grasp. I think the easiest way to sum it up is by looking back. Way back. Before there were calculators and scales that measured in exact grams.

Many, many years ago we learned to make beer, wine, and mead. By leaving any kind of sweet liquid to stand to its own devices, it began to ferment. The result was an alcoholic drink and people were delighted. At the time it was probably interpreted as "magic," but today we know better. Natural yeast exists everywhere, and this yeast wants to eat any kind of sugar. Sugar is found in starch. Starch is found in flour. By allowing yeast to come to life in a mixture of flour and water that is just left to stand, we get something that we've come to call sourdough. This is because over time the pH value of the flour mixture falls due to natural lactic acid bacteria that produce lactic acid and acetic acid. If we take our time and show a little patience, we can maintain this sourdough and use it just like regular yeast. The result, or reward, is bread that tastes so much better because we let it proof for a long time and develop complex, deep, sour flavors.

That's sourdough in a nutshell, and also proof that I'm not a wizard. I'm a guy of average talent. I didn't get good grades in high school. I enjoy hard rock. And now I bake bread in my garage. So if I can bake sourdough bread, you can too!

That's why my ambition with this book is that it be easy to understand and help anyone who wants to learn how to bake good sourdough bread at home, while leaving room for a lot of delicious recipes. Because that's really where the magic happens. When we explore all the goodness found in the grains, groats, and various flours. The variety, the breadth, and thus the simplicity of achieving fantastic flavors with small means and by making small changes.

Here we'll focus on the most important thing—baking without overanalyzing and overthinking. You'll get the answers anyway... By baking. You'll begin to see connections and piece together your own manual, in your head and in your fingers. Baking sourdough bread isn't rocket science, even though I can sometimes make it sound that way. It's just a matter of sticking to a few simple rules. And we'll start with the most important thing for making delicious bread—the sourdough!

Sourdough school

"Flour, water, and patience"

UNIT
ON
TARE
Max.5000g d=1g

Starting a sourdough

It takes about a week to start a sourdough, but it's really only a few minutes of work per day. The work involves mixing flour and water in a glass jar and letting it stand. Then you scrape most of the contents out of the jar and fill it with new flour and water. Every time you do that, you're feeding the sourdough. Flour, water, and time. That's all you need. If you don't give the sourdough time, you won't get any sourdough... Simple as that.

There's really only one parameter that's important for your sourdough. The sourdough must proof.

The sourdough must therefore become larger in volume in order to work. If the sourdough proofs, your bread dough will also proof. However, I want to point out that it's unimportant how the nascent sourdough behaves in its first five days. It can proof, bubble, stratify, and live its own life. It doesn't matter. I'll come back to why.

To easily see whether the sourdough is proofing, we use a glass jar with a lid and a rubber band to show the current level of the sourdough. To give some kind of reference, a typical applesauce jar is good, they're often a little larger and hold about 25 fluid ounces (750 ml). It's important not to use a jar that's too small.

You'll need:
Glass jar
Rubber band
Hard spatula
Scale that measures in grams or ounces
Flour
Water

Tip: Use organic flour when starting your sourdough. Organic flour contains more microorganisms—a prerequisite for the sourdough to start bubbling and come to life.

Also, get a jar or bowl and mix together about 90 percent bread flour and 10 percent wholemeal rye flour. The ratio between the flour types doesn't have to be exact, but the majority must be wheat. We do this because it's easier to scoop flour from one container into the "sourdough jar" than to dig into two bags. You'll need to feed your sourdough at regular intervals, so mix up plenty—a few pounds/kilos. This will now be your flour mixture, or the food that you'll use to feed your sourdough.

Tip: I always use weights in grams when baking. For the international version of this book, we've converted the gram measurements into ounces. However, you'll notice that for some very small measures such as 2 g, there is no ounce equivalent, simply because there is no ounce measurement small enough. Therefore, if your scales can weigh in grams, it's better to use that setting. In the US, it's very common to use volume-based measurements, such as cups. However, the reason I don't use volume measurements is because a cup of flour can vary greatly in weight depending on how compact or porous the flour is.

Sourdough—Day by day

Day 1, morning. Mix 1¾ ounces (50 g) of flour (from your flour mixture) with 1¾ ounces (50 g) of cold tap water in a glass jar with a lid. Stir thoroughly with the spatula so that all the flour dissolves in the water. Scrape down the inside of the jar so you can see how big and tall your future sourdough gets. Place your rubber band at the top level of the mixture. Leave the lid slightly loose as the sourdough will produce gas that needs to be released. Leave the jar on the countertop where you can easily see it, at normal room temperature. It doesn't need to be in a warm place, but it shouldn't be too cold. Leave to stand for 2 days.

Day 3, morning. Scrape 80–90 percent of the contents (which we can now call sourdough) out of the jar. This is a rule going forward: Every time you feed your sourdough, it also means you have to scrape out the majority of the existing sourdough and throw it away. Feed with 1¾ ounces (50 g) of flour and 1¾ ounces (50 g) of water. Stir. Adjust the rubber band if necessary.

Remember to keep the inside of the sourdough jar clean so that you can use the rubber band to see how much the sourdough has increased in volume.

Day 4, morning. Scrape out and re-feed with 1¾ ounces (50 g) of flour and 1¾ ounces (50 g) of water.

Day 5, morning. Scrape out and re-feed with 1¾ ounces (50 g) of flour and 1¾ ounces (50 g) of water.

Day 6, morning. Scrape out and re-feed with 1¾ ounces (50 g) of flour and 1¾ ounces (50 g) of water.

Starting on day 6, we'll start looking at our sourdough both morning and evening. We're looking to see that the sourdough is proofing consistently after each feeding. This means that the sourdough increases in volume and preferably doubles in size after each feeding. That's what I mean by consistent proofing—the sourdough behaves the same way all the time. If the sourdough does that, we will start feeding it twice a day, morning and evening.

If the sourdough doesn't rise in the evening, we'll continue to feed our sourdough once a day until we see it rise in the evening. It may therefore take a few more days before it's time to start evening feeds.

Day 6, evening. If the sourdough has doubled in size, we scrape it out and feed it again.

Day 7, morning. Scrape out and feed again.

Day 7, evening. If the sourdough has doubled in size, we scrape it out and feed it again.

Once the sourdough is proofing consistently after each feeding and you've fed the sourdough twice a day for two days, the sourdough is ready to use. If the sourdough stops doubling in the morning or evening during either of these two days, give the sourdough more time to establish itself. Return to feeding only once in the morning and wait for it to double by the evening for the "signal" that it's time to start feeding twice a day.

Day 8, morning. Scrape out and feed as much as you need for your bake. (This is assuming the sourdough has doubled in size and been fed twice a day for two full days.)

Baxtran
SS
0.385
OK
-0- -T- lb.oz lb.lb kg g

I wrote earlier that the sourdough must proof, and that this is the only thing you should look for. I then wrote that it doesn't matter whether your sourdough proofs or not during the first five days. Contradictory, right? But there's a very logical explanation.

In its first few days of life, this is what happens to a newly started sourdough: The sourdough is exposed to hundreds or thousands of microorganisms and bacteria that are fighting to gain a foothold. If you zoom in with a microscope, you'll see a small world war going on in the jar. That's why sourdough can bubble, stratify, or change smell from day to day. What happens after about five days is that yeast and lactic acid bacteria take hold and become dominant. The unwanted bacteria die out because the lactic acid bacteria have lowered the pH value (or simply made the environment acidic) and therefore the yeast can thrive. If the sourdough is left unfed for too long, it will become *too* acidic, which is why we start feeding it twice a day. This balances the pH and gives the sourdough, or yeast, new food in the form of new flour and water.

Five or six days is a reasonable amount of time for the flour mixture to become a working sourdough. However, it's completely impossible to say that it will take exactly that many days—natural microorganisms behave differently in different environments.

Taking your time when starting your sourdough will help you avoid a lot of headaches and rock-hard frisbees once you start baking. I promise that you'll benefit from it in the end and have a positive experience with sourdough baking. A good sourdough is the key to everything. Look after it and it'll give you amazing bread.

Maintain your sourdough

I mentioned that the sourdough must proof consistently after each feeding so you know that it's working properly. This is largely about you also being consistent with how you feed the sourdough. If you feed the sourdough consistently, morning and evening, I promise you that in time the sourdough will proof consistently. However, if you're lazy and skip feeding the sourdough, there's a great risk that the sourdough will stop proofing. Remember that. Be kind to your sourdough, and it'll be kind to you.

When you've used your sourdough to make bread dough and aren't planning to bake for another week or two, you can let it rest. Then it's perfectly fine to screw the lid on tightly and place the sourdough in the refrigerator. It can stay there for quite a long time without going bad, but it shouldn't be left there untouched for longer than a month. It doesn't matter what condition the sourdough is in when you place it in the refrigerator, whether it's freshly made or not. It also doesn't matter how much sourdough the jar contains. The sourdough will become cold and sour in the refrigerator.

When it's time to bake next time, simply take out the sourdough and do just as usual—scrape out the majority and feed it. What you need to make sure of now, just like during the start-up phase, is that the sourdough doubles in size *consistently* after each feeding before you use it for baking. It usually takes a few feedings to get the sourdough going again after it has been in the refrigerator. This is simply because the sourdough has been "sleeping" and the yeast is inactive.

I usually recommend feeding the sourdough *at least* twice before a new bake if the sourdough has been in the refrigerator. This means that if I plan to bake next Saturday and the sourdough has been in the fridge all week, I'll take it out on *Friday evening*. Scrape out and feed. On *Saturday morning,* the sourdough will hopefully have come to life. So then I scrape it out and feed it again. Around lunchtime, the sourdough will hopefully have doubled in size and be ready to use.

It takes roughly 4 to 8 hours for sourdough that is left out at room temperature and fed regularly to double in size. This largely depends on how warm it is in the kitchen, what time of year it is, and the temperature of the water you use. If it's warm it goes faster, if it's cool it goes slower. This means that if you want to get started and bake as quickly as possible, feed the sourdough with water that's slightly warmer. The same goes for your bread dough—the warmer it is, the faster it will proof. As a rule, I never go above 82°F (28°C) for either sourdough or bread dough.

After feeding, you have a relatively long time in which you can use your sourdough. By that I mean when the yeast will still work well. I would say somewhere around 12 hours after feeding, but this also depends largely on the temperature. A sourdough that is very warm proofs and becomes good before quickly going bad—quicker than a cool sourdough. It's pretty easy to see with the naked eye when it's good or bad. When the sourdough is making its way up inside the jar, it's great. When it starts to go down, it still works. Once the sourdough has completely sunk, it will start to become watery and much more acidic again. At this point, it's not recommended to use it for baking. A refeed

is often what's needed. The reason I recommend feeding in the morning and baking in the middle of the day is because the yeast is most active when it's still making its way up inside the jar. The sourdough itself is also mild in its acidity, which is my preference when it comes to the taste of the finished bread.

A final tip: It's almost impossible to feed a sourdough too often or too much. The longer the sourdough sits unfed, the more acidic it becomes. Once the sourdough becomes too acidic, the yeast will not do well. So make sure the sourdough is fresh. I recommend feeding a sourdough that is left out at room temperature twice a day, morning and evening. Just like we did earlier in the book when we started our sourdough. However, this requires a lot of work. If you're not going to bake, it's better to leave it in the refrigerator when you're not using it.

Baking your first bread

"Practice makes perfect"

OFF
ON
SET
(0~9)
lb.oz
lb.lb
kg
g
OK

Tools

The following tools are good to have when baking sourdough bread. You'll see for yourself that some things are essential, while others are perhaps more of a luxury. If you're not sure that you want to dedicate your life to sourdough baking, you might be able to borrow some of the tools from a relative or friend.

Oven-safe pot with lid. I use a combo cast iron pot about 10 inches (26 cm) in diameter. An oval ceramic pot like the one you often cook a whole chicken in also works well.

Dough bowl with lid or kitchen towel (to cover the bowl with). The bowls I use at home hold 1 gallon (4 liters), which is enough for most of my recipes. It's always better to have a bowl that's too big than one that's too small.

Dough scrapers. One straight-edged in hard metal, and one with a curved edge in soft plastic, known as a dough card, to get all the dough out of the bowl.

Proofing baskets with covers or a linen/tea towel. It doesn't really matter whether they're oblong or round. It's more about what you prefer to look at. According to their specifications, my baskets hold around 26–28 ounces (750–800 g) of dough, or around 3 pints (1.5 liters). The round ones are 8 inches (20 cm) in diameter and the oblong ones are approximately 10 inches (25 cm) long and 5 ½ inches (14 cm) wide. Most of my recipes require two proofing baskets.

Oven mitts. A pot that is in the oven gets hot and heavy, so you need a pair of sensible oven mitts to protect your hands.

Paring knife or razor blade. There are many different paring knives to choose from. I think the most important thing is that you can replace the blades on the knife, as they quickly become dull.

Electric scales that measure in grams or ounces. Make sure your scales are not undersized. A bowl and dough for two loaves of bread weighs a lot, so a scale that can measure at least up to 11 pounds (5 kg) is a good benchmark.

Baking steel. A thick steel sheet that is preheated in the oven. Some of my recipes for larger breads such as baguettes require this.

Baking stone. Works in the same way as a baking steel. If you're going to invest in one or the other, I'd recommend a baking steel over a baking stone.

Bread peel/pizza peel. For shoveling larger breads or rolls—which are not baked in a pot—into the oven.

Basic recipe with wheat & rye

Your first and most important bread. Feel free to make this bread several times before moving on to the other recipes.

The recipe can be seen as a template for how to make all breads, with some modification. This bread is a good one to practice on. The result is an airy and delicious sourdough bread with a pleasant, mild acidity.

Weight		Ingredients	Baker's percentage
total flour weight: 28 ¼ oz.	(800 g)	for 2 breads	100 %
2 ¾ oz.	(80 g)	wholemeal rye flour	10 %
25 ⅓ oz.	(720 g)	bread flour	90 %
21¼ oz.	(600 g)	water	75 %
5 ⅔ oz.	(160 g)	sourdough	20 %
½ oz.	(16 g)	salt	2 %

For all the recipes in this book, I will refer to a baking schedule with times. The times should be seen as a tool, so that you can see how much time there is between each step.

If you want to bake a double batch of the recipe, feed your sourdough with twice as much flour and water so that you get double the amount of sourdough. You can create as much sourdough as you want from the tiny leftovers in your jar. It'll just take slightly longer for the sourdough to double in size. If you want to bake half a batch, halve the recipe.

For this recipe, we use the two types of flour we used when creating the sourdough—bread flour and wholemeal rye flour. The percentage on the right is called the *baker's percentage*. This is a method of calculation that many bakers use to easily see the ratio between ingredients. The total quantity of dry flour is always 100 percent, so the flour in the sourdough does not count. Other ingredients are put in relation to the weight of the flour.

Baking schedule and method

07:00 Feed the dough and measure water
On the day we're going to make the dough, we often need a little more sourdough than what results from the usual feeding 1 ¾ + 1 ¾ = 3 ½ ounces (50 + 50 = 100 g). Scrape out and feed with 3 ½ ounces (100 g) of flour and 3 ½ ounces (100 g) of water. With what little you have left in the jar, this gives you just over 7 ounces (200 g) of sourdough. You need 5 ⅔ ounces (160 g) for this recipe, so this will be perfect. Adjust the rubber band to the new level of the sourdough.

At the same time, weigh out the water 21 ¼ ounces (600 g) for the bread dough in a separate jug so that it's at room temperature just in time for making the dough. Try to make this a routine. It's much easier to knead dough in lukewarm water than in cold water straight from the tap. This will help the dough proof a little faster and make it easier for you to see how it's developing. If you forget to weigh out water in the morning, heat cold water in the microwave or on the stove, to a maximum of 82°F (28°C).

12:00 Mix the dough

Pour almost all the water (19 ¾ ounces/560 g), the sourdough (which should now be about double in size after feeding), and the flour into a bowl and mix by hand. Save a small splash of water (1½ ounces/40 g). Mix well until no dry lumps of flour remain. Mixing for a minute or so is usually enough. Cover the dough with a lid or kitchen towel after each step to prevent the dough from drying out.

12:30 Mix in the salt

Mix in the salt and the last splash of water by hand. The small splash of water helps distribute the salt evenly through the dough. Mix for a minute or two. There's no need to knead. Cover with a lid/kitchen towel.

Tip: If you're not going to bake any more in the next few days, it's no problem to place the sourdough jar in the refrigerator. However, if you want to make

new dough tomorrow or the day after, leave the sourdough out at room temperature and feed it as usual morning and evening.

13:00 Fold the dough for the first time
This step is called folding the dough. With a wet hand, grab the outer edge of the dough in the bowl and fold it over itself. Rotate the bowl a quarter turn and continue folding, over and over again, until you've folded the entire dough over itself. Then cover with a kitchen towel or lid. It usually takes four or five folds like this to get through the entire dough. Folding helps to break up the dough, even out the temperature and build some structure, or act as a gentle kind of kneading. This is done a total of four times, once every half an hour. After the fourth fold, let the dough rest until it's time for the next step (preshape).

13:30 Fold the dough a second time

14:00 Fold the dough a third time

14:30 Fold the dough a fourth time

16:30 Preshape (or ball) the dough
By now your bread dough should be significantly larger and airier. Surface air bubbles should be visible and it should bulge upward. Since we're making two loaves, you need to divide the dough in two. Do this by tipping the dough bowl over and scraping the contents onto the counter. Then use your dough scraper to divide the dough in two. Having a small bowl of water close at hand is a good idea. Then you can just lightly wet the dough scraper and your hands to prevent everything from getting too sticky.

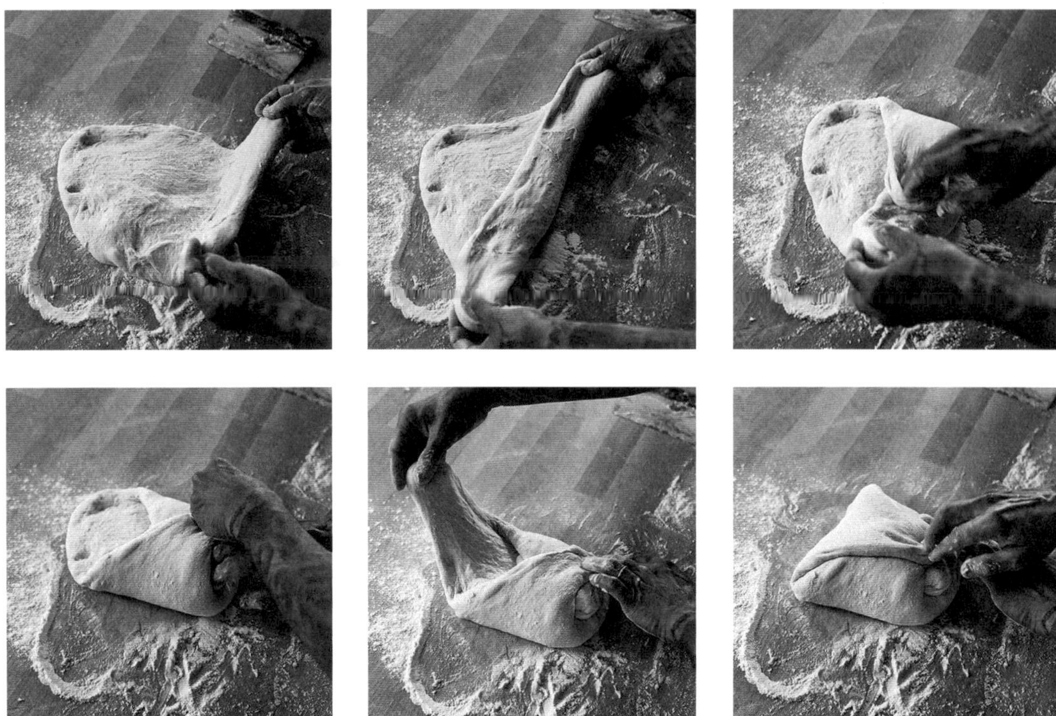

The whole point of the process is to make two nice balls of dough with a smooth, taut surface. You need to move the dough scraper under the dough, toward the counter, while applying a little pressure with your other hand on top of the dough and making small circular movements to form … balls. This step is one of the most difficult at the beginning. It will be messy and feel unfamiliar. The most important thing is that you don't handle the dough too much and are satisfied when you have some kind of a ball. It'll get easier in the next step when you can use flour.

17:00 Final shape
It's time to get the dough into the proofing baskets, place them in the refrigerator, and keep your fingers crossed until the next day. Prepare your proofing baskets by flouring them thoroughly. If your baskets don't have covers, place a kitchen towel in them as you flour them.

Generously flour the dough balls on the counter. Then take your dough scraper and run it under one of the balls. Try to go around the entire ball until you feel it start to release from the counter. Then turn the entire thing over and place it face down on the counter. The messier side is now face up.

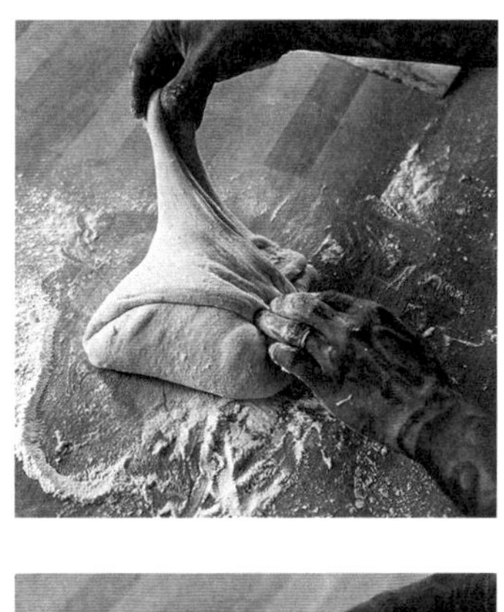

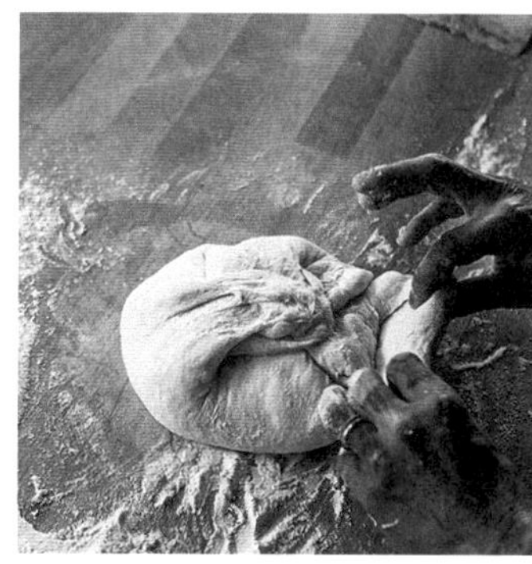

Shaping for an oval proofing basket

Gently pull the dough out at the edges so that the dough becomes even and oval. Take the bottom edge of the dough and fold it up about an inch (a few centimeters) over itself. Then take the right and left edges and fold them over the dough until you get something that looks like an open envelope. Close the "envelope" by folding down the top edge of the dough. Then take the two top corners of the dough and fold these down over the dough as well and press lightly so that they stick. You then take the bottom edge of the dough, which is pointing toward your stomach, and roll it over the entire dough away from you. Finally, pull the entire dough toward you and the counter to seal, or close, the underside of the dough. You should now have a small oval package of dough in front of you. Pick up the entire package and place it in one of your floured proofing baskets with the smooth surface facing down. Where all the dough sides meet is called a seam. Have the seam on show, face up. Do the same with the other dough.

Shaping for a round proofing basket

Fold the dough in toward the middle. From the left, right, top, and bottom. Then do the same thing once more with the four points you've made. Then turn the dough over so that the seam is facing the counter and pull the entire dough toward you and the counter so that the seam is sealed underneath. Pick the dough up and place it with the smooth side down in the basket and the seam face up.

It may be advisable to put a plastic bag or similar over the proofing baskets so that they don't take on unwanted odors from other foods in the refrigerator. This also prevents further dehydration. Place the baskets at the bottom of your refrigerator, where it's coldest.

The next day—bake

It's now time to bake your bread. The day you choose to bake is up to you, but letting the

loaves rest in the refrigerator for at least one night is recommended.

Place a pot on a rack or sheet pan at the bottom of the oven. If it's too high up, the excess heat can burn the top of the bread and it can be difficult to remove the lid from the pot. Set the oven to 480°F (250°C), using the top and bottom elements. No fan is needed. Let the oven and pot preheat for 1 hour.

After 1 hour, take one of your doughs out of the refrigerator and turn it out onto a sheet of baking parchment. Cut off any excess paper that sticks out, but make sure to save some on the sides so you can easily lift the dough using the paper. Make a score ¼ inch deep (2–3 mm) across the bread with a paring knife or razor blade. Using oven mitts, remove the pot from the oven and place it on a heat-resistant surface. Remove the lid. Then place your dough in the pot using the excess baking paper. It doesn't matter if the baking paper sticks up a little. Put the lid on the pot and place it back in the oven. Reduce the oven temperature to 450°F (230°C). After 20 minutes, remove the lid from the pot and continue baking for another 20 minutes, so that the bread will have baked for a total of 40 minutes.

Tip: Remember to be careful when lifting the lid because very hot steam will be released. So turn your head away when you do this.

20 minutes with the lid on, and 20 minutes with it off. If you want to be sure that the bread is done, use a probe thermometer. The internal temperature should measure 205°F (96°C) or more. If you don't have a thermometer, you can tap the underside of the bread with your finger. It should sound hollow when it's done.

Take the bread out and place it on a rack, otherwise it may get a little soggy on the bottom as it will continue to release moisture. Place the pot in the oven again, turn up the temperature back up to 480°F (250°C), and repeat with the next loaf after about 20 minutes once the pot and oven have heated up again.

Let the freshly baked bread rest for about 30 minutes before cutting it. It needs to dry out and "settle" a bit first. Otherwise, there's the risk it will be a little chewy when you cut into it.

Things to bear in mind before you start

Baking schedule and temperature

The recipes are designed to be started in the middle of the day, 12:00. This gives you time to feed your sourdough in the morning, about 5 hours before you start making the dough. This will give you a pleasant and mild sourdough with active yeast. If you'd rather start the bread dough at 17:00, that's perfectly fine, but then it's up to you to time your sourdough so that it's ready when you want it. I'd suggest that you keep it a little cooler if you do your feeding in the morning or do an extra feeding in the middle of the day.

The times are provided as a guide, so you know approximately how long it will take to finish the dough. But you have to keep in mind that it is the temperature that controls the proofing and thus when the dough is "ready." Proofing is usually quicker in the summer and takes longer in the winter. This means that in the height of summer, you may have to put the bread dough in the refrigerator as early as the four-hour mark, while in winter it often needs up to seven hours to get nice and big before going into the refrigerator.

In time, you'll learn to follow your bread dough and judge for yourself when it's ready. You'll see and feel it. But all this, and much more, you'll find out for yourself in due course.

Gluten quality and hydration

The gluten quality of flour can vary slightly even if you bought the exact same brand as last time. This means that a flour can sometimes be weaker than you're used to. In which case, you may need to hold back a little on the amount of water, the hydration. That's one of the reasons why you should save some water (about 1½ ounces/40 g) when mixing your dough. You should never add more flour to a recipe. It's always about using more or less water. Sometimes the dough becomes loose enough during the first mixing, and you don't need to add the last bit of water. In this way, you can easily modify the recipes by about 5 percent hydration up or down, which is usually what's required for the dough to turn out as intended.

If this is your first time trying a recipe or if you're baking with a flour that you've never used before, follow the recipes to the letter. Then the next time you make the same recipe, you'll have a reference. If the previous dough was too hard and sticky, you'll probably need a little more water. If the dough became super loose, so that it was almost impossible to work with it, it might be a good idea to reduce the hydration a little.

Choice of flour

I almost exclusively use artisanal flour when I bake bread. Many of these flours can be difficult to find in the grocery store. Don't let this limit you, and use the flours you can get your hands on. You can replace all sifted white flour with bread flour. All the wholemeal flours I use can be replaced with any other wholemeal flour, such as graham or spelt wholemeal flour, and instead of landrace rye flour you can use standard rye flour. Although it won't be exactly the same bread as in the recipe, it'll still be amazingly good.

In brief, I'd give the following advice when you start the recipes:

- Sourdough is optimal for use in bread dough once it has roughly doubled in size and increases in volume after each feeding.
- It's better to use a strong white flour, such as bread flour, than a weaker white flour at first.
- Use a little less water and work your way up as you become more accustomed to baking.
- The temperature determines when the dough is ready. The schedule is therefore more of a reference rather than a rule.

Simple breads

The recipes in this book are divided into five sections: *simple breads*, *breads with extra ingredients*, *breads with porridge, groats, and whole grains*, *sweet breads*, and *stale bread & other tasty recipes*. We'll start with bread that works for all occasions—breakfast, lunch, dinner, and everything in between. The very first recipes introduce you to the most common types of flour, which you can find in any grocery store. We'll also experiment with a few additional ingredients in and on the bread to get a feel for the process. These recipes are a good place to start, not only because they put delicious bread on the table, but also because they teach you the basics of baking well.

Once you've got the hang of the basics, you can use my recipes as a starting point and experiment to your heart's content!

Wheat bread

Light and delicious. A typical levain bread, which simply means sourdough bread.

Weight		Ingredients	Baker's percentage
total flour weight: 28 ¼ oz.	(800 g)	for 2 breads	100 %
3 ½ oz.	(100 g)	graham flour	12.5 %
24 ¾ oz.	(700 g)	bread flour	87.5 %
21 ¼ oz.	(600 g)	water	75 %
5 ⅔ oz.	(160 g)	sourdough	20 %
½ oz.	(16 g)	salt	2 %

12:00 Mix almost all the water, sourdough, and flour together in a bowl. Cover with a lid / kitchen towel.

12:30 Mix in the salt and the remaining water. Cover with a lid / kitchen towel.

13:00 Fold the dough over itself. Take one edge of the dough, pull it up, and fold it over itself. Rotate the bowl a quarter turn and repeat until you've folded all the dough. Cover with a lid / kitchen towel.

13:30 Fold the dough a second time.

14:00 Fold the dough a third time.

14:30 Fold the dough a fourth time.

16:30 Divide the dough in two. Preshape.

17:00 Final shape. Place a plastic bag over the baskets and place in the refrigerator.

Bake the next day. Preheat your baking sheet and the pot with the lid on for 1 hour in an oven set to 480°F (250°C), using the top and bottom elements. Score the bread, place it in the pot, and put the lid on. Reduce the heat to 450°F (230°C). After 20 minutes, remove the lid and bake for another 20 minutes. Repeat the procedure for the second bread.

Wheat with sunflower hearts

This bread is very tasty when covered with sunflower hearts, which take on a wonderfully toasted flavor when baked in the oven.

Weight	Ingredients	Baker's percentage
total flour weight: 28 ¼ oz. (800 g)	for 2 breads	100 %
3 ½ oz. (100 g)	graham flour	12.5 %
24 ¾ oz. (700 g)	bread flour	87.5 %
21 ¼ oz. (600 g)	water	75 %
5 ⅔ oz. (160 g)	sourdough	20 %
½ oz. (16 g)	salt	2 %
	+ sunflower hearts to cover the bread with	

12:00 Mix almost all the water, sourdough, and flour together in a bowl. Cover with a lid / kitchen towel.

12:30 Mix in the salt and the remaining water. Cover with a lid / kitchen towel.

13:00 Fold the dough over itself. Take one edge of the dough, pull it up, and fold it over itself. Rotate the bowl a quarter turn and repeat until you've folded all the dough. Cover with a lid / kitchen towel.

13:30 Fold the dough a second time.

14:00 Fold the dough a third time.

14:30 Fold the dough a fourth time.

16:30 Divide the dough in two. Preshape.

17:00 Final shape. Prepare a plate or tray with the sunflower hearts. After the final shape, spray or brush the top of the dough with water and roll in the sunflower seeds. Then place the dough in proofing baskets with the seam face up. You don't need to flour the proofing baskets as the sunflower hearts act as your "non-stick coating." Place a plastic bag over the baskets and place in the refrigerator.

Bake the next day. Preheat your baking sheet and the pot with the lid on for 1 hour in an oven set to 480°F (250°C), using the top and bottom elements. Score the bread, place it in the pot, and put the lid on. Reduce the heat to 450°F (230°C). After 20 minutes, remove the lid and bake for another 20 minutes. Repeat the procedure for the second bread.

Rye bread

This slightly punchy rye-based bread has a special aroma. When a hard crust forms during baking, it has a particularly intense flavor.

Weight	Ingredients	Baker's percentage
total flour weight: 28 ¼ oz. (800 g)	for 2 breads	100 %
5 ⅔ oz. (160 g)	wholemeal rye flour	20 %
11¼ oz. (320 g)	sifted rye flour	40 %
11¼ oz. (320 g)	bread flour	40 %
21¼ oz. (600 g)	water	75 %
5 ½ oz. (160 g)	sourdough	20 %
½ oz. (16 g)	salt	2 %

12:00 Mix almost all the water, sourdough, and flour together in a bowl. Cover with a lid/kitchen towel.

12:30 Mix in the salt and the remaining water. Cover with a lid/kitchen towel.

13:00 Fold the dough over itself. Take one edge of the dough, pull it up, and fold it over itself. Rotate the bowl a quarter turn and repeat until you've folded all the dough. Cover with a lid/kitchen towel.

13:30 Fold the dough a second time.

14:00 Fold the dough a third time.

14:30 Fold the dough a fourth time.

16:30 Divide the dough in two. Preshape.

17:00 Final shape. Place a plastic bag over the baskets and place in the refrigerator.

Bake the next day. Preheat your baking sheet and the pot with the lid on for 1 hour in an oven set to 480°F (250°C), using the top and bottom elements. Score the bread, place it in the pot, and put the lid on. Reduce the heat to 450°F (230°C). After 20 minutes, remove the lid and bake for another 20 minutes. Repeat the procedure for the second bread.

Rye with raisins

I absolutely love the punchy, slightly tart rye combined with the sweet raisins. Every morning when we eat this bread, my son wants to "look" at my sandwich. "Look" means pick out the raisins, eat them, and then give me back a raisin-free sandwich.

Weight		Ingredients	Baker's percentage
total flour weight: 28 ¼ oz.	(800 g)	for 2 breads	100 %
5 ⅔ oz.	(160 g)	wholemeal rye flour	20 %
11 ¼ oz.	(320 g)	sifted rye flour	40 %
11 ¼ oz.	(320 g)	bread flour	40 %
21 ¼ oz.	(600 g)	water	75 %
5 ½ oz.	(160 g)	sourdough	20 %
½ oz.	(16 g)	salt	2 %
4 ½ oz.	(120 g)	raisins	15 %

11:00 Place the raisins in a small bowl and pour just enough water (from the total amount of water in the recipe) to cover them. You usually need about the same amount of water by weight as dried fruit.

12:00 Mix the remaining water, sourdough, and flour in a bowl. Cover with a lid / kitchen towel.

12:30 Mix in the salt and the soaked raisins, including the water they're in. Cover with a lid / kitchen towel.

13:00 Fold the dough over itself. Take one edge of the dough, pull it up, and fold it over itself. Rotate the bowl a quarter turn and repeat until you've folded all the dough. Cover with a lid / kitchen towel.

13:30 Fold the dough a second time.

14:00 Fold the dough a third time.

14:30 Fold the dough a fourth time.

16:30 Divide the dough in two. Preshape.

17:00 Final shape. Place a plastic bag over the baskets and place in the refrigerator.

Bake the next day. Preheat your baking sheet and the pot with the lid on for 1 hour in an oven set to 480°F (250°C), using the top and bottom elements. Score the bread, place it in the pot, and put the lid on. Reduce the heat to 450°F (230°C). After 20 minutes, remove the lid and bake for another 20 minutes. Repeat the procedure for the second bread.

Spelt rolls

Light, airy spelt rolls that are extra tasty when topped with mixed seeds, offering a delightful nutty crunch with every bite.

Weight		**Ingredients**	**Baker's percentage**
total flour weight: 28 ¼ oz.	(800 g)	for around 16 rolls	100 %
28 ¼ oz.	(800 g)	sifted durum flour	100 %
21 ¼ oz.	(600 g)	water	75 %
5 ½ oz.	(160 g)	sourdough	20 %
½ oz.	(16 g)	salt	2 %
		+ seeds to top the rolls with, e. g., sunflower hearts, sesame seeds, and flax seeds	

12:00 Mix almost all the water, sourdough, and flour together in a bowl. Cover with a lid / kitchen towel.

12:30 Mix in the salt and the remaining water. Cover with a lid / kitchen towel.

13:00 Fold the dough over itself. Take one edge of the dough, pull it up, and fold it over itself. Rotate the bowl a quarter turn and repeat until you've folded all the dough. Cover with a lid / kitchen towel.

13:30 Fold the dough a second time.

14:00 Fold the dough a third time.

14:30 Fold the dough a fourth time.

16:30 Place a plastic bag over the bowl and place in the refrigerator until the next day.

Bake the next day. Place a baking steel or sheet pan in the middle of the oven. At the same time, place an oven-safe dish at the bottom of the oven. Preheat the oven to 480°F (250°C) for 1 hour, using the top and bottom elements.

Flour the counter well and roll out all the dough. Pull it to get a roughly even rectangle.

Cover the top of the dough with seeds. They'll stick easily because the dough is sticky on top. If there's flour on top, spray the dough with a little water so that the seeds stick. (If you want rolls without any seeds, it's best to flour the top of the dough before you start cutting out the rolls, as then the dough scraper and your hands won't stick as much.)

Using the dough scraper, slice into small squares and place on two sheets of baking parchment. You can choose the size for yourself.

Then, using a peel, slide the entire sheet of baking parchment into the oven and onto your preheated baking steel or sheet pan. Pour ½–1 cup (100–200 ml) of boiling water into the baking dish and close the oven door. Bake for about 15 minutes. I like to bake rolls hot and fast to get an airy roll with a lovely thin crust, but you'll need to check the underside of the rolls to make sure they don't burn. If you're unsure, you can lower the temperature to 450°F (230°C) and bake for 20–25 minutes instead.

Repeat with the rolls on the second sheet of baking parchment.

Sifted rye flour rolls

Simple and tasty rolls with a hint of extra flavor. Perfect for a hearty breakfast, as a side dish to a soup, or for a barbecue.

Weight	Ingredients	Baker's percentage
total flour weight: 28 ¼ oz. (800 g)	for around 16 rolls	100 %
28 ¼ oz. (800 g)	sifted rye flour	100 %
21 ¼ oz. (600 g)	water	75 %
5 ½ oz. (160 g)	sourdough	20 %
½ oz. (16 g)	salt	2 %

12:00 Mix almost all the water, sourdough, and flour together in a bowl. Cover with a lid/kitchen towel.

12:30 Mix in the salt and the remaining water. Cover with a lid/kitchen towel.

13:00 Fold the dough over itself. Take one edge of the dough, pull it up, and fold it over itself. Rotate the bowl a quarter turn and repeat until you've folded all the dough. Cover with a lid/kitchen towel.

13:30 Fold the dough a second time.

14:00 Fold the dough a third time.

14:30 Fold the dough a fourth time.

16:30 Put a plastic bag over the dough bowl and place in the refrigerator until the next day.

Bake the next day. Place a baking steel or sheet pan in the middle of the oven. At the same time, place an oven-safe dish at the bottom of the oven. Preheat the oven to 480°F (250°C) for 1 hour, using the top and bottom elements.

Flour the counter well and roll out all the dough. Also flour the top of the dough to make it easier to work with. I like to flour the top of the dough with whole wheat rye flour because it looks nice, but wheat flour works just as well. Pull the dough to get a roughly even rectangle.

Using the dough scraper, slice into small squares and place on two sheets of baking parchment. You can choose the size for yourself.

Then, using a peel, slide the entire sheet of baking parchment into the oven and onto your preheated baking steel or sheet pan. Pour ½–1 cups (100–200 ml) of boiling water into your baking dish and close the oven door. Bake for about 15 minutes. I like to bake rolls hot and fast to get an airy roll with a lovely thin crust, but you'll need to check the underside of the rolls to make sure they don't burn. If you're unsure, lower the temperature to 450°F (230°C) and bake for 20–25 minutes instead.

Repeat with the rolls on the second sheet of baking parchment.

Coarse heritage bread

A coarser bread baked exclusively with heritage wheat flour. The old varieties vary as much as the regions where they grow. They enrich wheat diversity, and their full flavor perfectly suits sourdough.

Weight		Ingredients	Baker's percentage
total flour weight: 28 ¼ oz.	(800 g)	for 2 breads	100 %
14 oz.	(400 g)	wholemeal heritage wheat flour	50 %
14 oz.	(400 g)	sifted heritage wheat flour	50 %
21¼ oz.	(600 g)	water	75 %
5 ½ oz.	(160 g)	sourdough	20 %
½ oz.	(16 g)	salt	2 %

12:00 Mix almost all the water, sourdough, and flour together in a bowl. Cover with a lid / kitchen towel.

12:30 Mix in the salt and the remaining water. Cover with a lid / kitchen towel.

13:00 Fold the dough over itself. Take one edge of the dough, pull it up, and fold it over itself. Rotate the bowl a quarter turn and repeat until you've folded all the dough. Cover with a lid / kitchen towel.

13:30 Fold the dough a second time.

14:00 Fold the dough a third time.

14:30 Fold the dough a fourth time.

16:30 Divide the dough in two. Preshape.

17:00 Final shape. Place a plastic bag over the baskets and place in the refrigerator.

Bake the next day. Preheat your baking sheet and the pot with the lid on for 1 hour in an oven set to 480°F (250°C), using the top and bottom elements. Score the bread, place it in the pot, and put the lid on. Reduce the heat to 450°F (230°C). After 20 minutes, remove the lid and bake for another 20 minutes. Repeat the procedure for the second bread.

Einkorn bread

Einkorn bread is a clear favorite. With its orange hue and delicious flavor, this loaf of bread is unique.

Weight		Ingredients	Baker's percentage
total flour weight: 28 ¼ oz.	(800 g)	for 2 breads	100 %
10 ½ oz.	(300 g)	wholemeal einkorn flour	37.5 %
6 ⅓ oz.	(180 g)	sifted einkorn flour	22.5 %
11¼ oz.	(320 g)	sifted heritage wheat flour	40 %
19 oz.	(540 g)	water	67.5 %
5 ½ oz.	(160 g)	sourdough	20 %
½ oz.	(16 g)	salt	2 %

12:00 Mix almost all the water, sourdough, and flour together in a bowl. Cover with a lid / kitchen towel.

12:30 Mix in the salt and the remaining water. Cover with a lid / kitchen towel.

13:00 Fold the dough over itself. Take one edge of the dough, pull it up, and fold it over itself. Rotate the bowl a quarter turn and repeat until you've folded all the dough. Cover with a lid / kitchen towel.

13:30 Fold the dough a second time.

14:00 Fold the dough a third time.

14:30 Fold the dough a fourth time.

16:30 Divide the dough in two. Preshape.

17:00 Final shape. Place a plastic bag over the baskets and place in the refrigerator.

Bake the next day. Preheat your baking sheet and the pot with the lid on for 1 hour in an oven set to 480°F (250°C), using the top and bottom elements. Score the bread, place it in the pot, and put the lid on. Reduce the heat to 450°F (230°C). After 20 minutes, remove the lid and bake for another 20 minutes. Repeat the procedure for the second bread.

Stina's einkorn

My wife fell in love with this bread when I made it once. "It melts in your mouth," she said after a few bites. And I can only agree. I use vortex-milled flour to make the bread as airy as possible, but regular wholemeal einkorn flour works just as well.

Weight		Ingredients	Baker's percentage
total flour weight: 28 ¼ oz.	(800 g)	for 2 breads	100 %
5 ⅔ oz.	(160 g)	vortex-milled wholemeal einkorn flour	20 %
22 ½ oz.	(640 g)	sifted heritage wheat flour	80 %
19 ¾ oz.	(560 g)	water	70 %
5 ½ oz.	(160 g)	sourdough	20 %
½ oz.	(16 g)	salt	2 %

12:00 Mix almost all the water, sourdough, and flour together in a bowl. Cover with a lid / kitchen towel.

12:30 Mix in the salt and the remaining water. Cover with a lid / kitchen towel.

13:00 Fold the dough over itself. Take one edge of the dough, pull it up, and fold it over itself. Rotate the bowl a quarter turn and repeat until you've folded all the dough. Cover with a lid / kitchen towel.

13:30 Fold the dough a second time.

14:00 Fold the dough a third time.

14:30 Fold the dough a fourth time.

16:30 Divide the dough in two. Preshape.

17:00 Final shape. Place a plastic bag over the baskets and place in the refrigerator.

Bake the next day. Preheat your baking sheet and the pot with the lid on for 1 hour in an oven set to 480°F (250°C), using the top and bottom elements. Score the bread, place it in the pot, and put the lid on. Reduce the heat to 450°F (230°C). After 20 minutes, remove the lid and bake for another 20 minutes. Repeat the procedure for the second bread.

Four kinds of rye

A flavorful, slightly coarse bread made with four types of rye. The rye bran is toasted before we bake with it to get a deeper flavor. Rye bran can be replaced with coarsely ground rye flour or finely ground rye groats.

Weight		Ingredients	Baker's percentage
total flour weight: 28 ¼ oz.	(800 g)	for 2 breads	100 %
5 ½ oz.	(160 g)	wholemeal landrace rye flour	20 %
5 ⅔ oz.	(160 g)	unblended sifted rye flour	20 %
2 ¾ oz.	(80 g)	wholemeal rye flour	10 %
14 oz.	(400 g)	sifted heritage wheat flour	50 %
22 ½ oz.	(640 g)	water	80 %
5 ½ oz.	(160 g)	sourdough	20 %
⅔ oz.	(18 g)	salt	2.25 %
1¾ oz.	(50 g)	toasted rye bran	6.25 %
+ 3 ½ oz.	(100 g)	water for scalding	

Toast the rye the night before you're going to make the dough. Spread out on a sheet pan and place in the oven for about 15 minutes at 350°F (175°C). Let the rye bran start to smoke and take on a nice color and aroma. Pour the rye bran into a bowl and then pour boiling water over it. Stir, put a lid on, and leave until the next day.

12:00 Mix almost all the water, sourdough, and flour together in a bowl. Cover with a lid / kitchen towel.

12:30 Mix in the salt, rye bran, and the remaining water. Cover with a lid / kitchen towel.

13:00 Fold the dough over itself. Take one edge of the dough, pull it up, and fold it over itself. Rotate the bowl a quarter turn and repeat until you've folded all the dough. Cover with a lid / kitchen towel.

13:30 Fold the dough a second time.

16:30 Divide the dough in two. Preshape.

17:00 This dough is so sticky that I usually forget the final shape and just flour the dough thoroughly and then place them into individual baskets. Place a plastic bag over the baskets and place in the refrigerator.

Bake the next day. Preheat your baking sheet and the pot with the lid on for 1 hour in an oven set to 480°F (250°C), using the top and bottom elements. Score the bread, place it in the pot, and put the lid on. Reduce the heat to 450°F (230°C). After 20 minutes, remove the lid and bake for another 20 minutes. Repeat the procedure for the second bread.

Grand levain

A big, beautiful loaf of bread. In the bakery, I make these loaves twice as big as regular loaves and use the entire recipe for one large loaf, but it's absolutely possible to achieve the same lovely appearance with two smaller loaves.

Weight		Ingredients	Baker's percentage
total flour weight: 28 ¼ oz.	(800 g)	for 2 breads	100 %
2 ¾ oz.	(80 g)	wholemeal landrace rye flour	10 %
7 oz.	(200 g)	stone-ground sifted spelt flour	25 %
9 ¼ oz.	(260 g)	sifted heritage wheat flour	32.5 %
9 ¼ oz.	(260 g)	bread flour	32.5 %
21 ¼ oz.	(600 g)	water	75 %
5 ½ oz.	(160 g)	sourdough	20 %
⅔ oz.	(18 g)	salt	2.25 %

12:00 Mix almost all the water, sourdough, and flour together in a bowl. Cover with a lid / kitchen towel.

12:30 Mix in the salt and the remaining water. Cover with a lid / kitchen towel.

13:00 Fold the dough over itself. Take one edge of the dough, pull it up, and fold it over itself. Rotate the bowl a quarter turn and repeat until you've folded all the dough. Cover with a lid / kitchen towel.

13:30 Fold the dough a second time.

14:00 Fold the dough a third time.

14:30 Fold the dough a fourth time.

16:30 Place a plastic bag over the dough bowl and place in the refrigerator until the next day.

Bake the next day. Place a baking steel or sheet pan in the middle of the oven. At the same time, place an oven-safe dish at the bottom of the oven. Preheat the oven to 480°F (250°C) for 1 hour, using the top and bottom elements.

Roll out the dough on the counter, divide it in two, and do a light preshape to make two fairly even balls. Let the dough rest for about 30 minutes.

Thoroughly flour the dough and the counter. Turn it so that the floured side is facing down and stretch it out a little so that the dough becomes rectangular. Fold in all the sides. Start with the long sides and finish with the short sides until you get something that looks a bit like a pierogi. Flour the seam quite generously so that it doesn't stick.

Use a dough scraper and your other hand to turn the entire dough over so that the seam is face down on the counter. Let the dough rest for 20 minutes. Do the same with the other dough.

Turn each dough onto a separate sheet of baking paper with the seam face up. Slide into the oven (without scoring) using a peel. Pour ½–1 cups (100–200 ml) of boiling water into your baking dish and close the oven door. Lower the heat to 450°F (230°C). Remove the baking dish with water after 20 minutes and bake for another 20 minutes. Repeat the procedure for the second bread. The idea with this method is to get a nice self-cracked bread that looks rustic and delicious.

Landrace breads

I make these breads twice as big as regular breads, so I use the entire recipe for one large bread. If it's difficult to find space in your home oven, I recommend doing as usual and baking two breads instead.

Weight		Ingredients	Baker's percentage
total flour weight: 28 ¼ oz.	(800 g)	for 2 breads	100 %
5 oz.	(140 g)	wholemeal landrace rye flour	17.5 %
5 oz.	(140 g)	unblended sifted rye flour	17.5 %
18 ⅓ oz.	(520 g)	sifted heritage wheat flour	65 %
21 ¾ oz.	(620 g)	water	77.5 %
5 ½ oz.	(160 g)	sourdough	20 %
⅔ oz.	(18 g)	salt	2.25 %

12:00 Mix almost all the water, sourdough, and flour together in a bowl. Cover with a lid / kitchen towel.

12:30 Mix in the salt and the remaining water. Cover with a lid / kitchen towel.

13:00 Fold the dough over itself. Take one edge of the dough, pull it up, and fold it over itself. Rotate the bowl a quarter turn and repeat until you've folded all the dough. Cover with a lid / kitchen towel.

13:30 Fold the dough a second time.

14:00 Fold the dough a third time.

14:30 Fold the dough a fourth time.

16:30 Divide the dough in two. Preshape.

17:00 Final shape. Place a plastic bag over the baskets and place in the refrigerator.

Bake the next day. Preheat your baking sheet and the pot with the lid on for 1 hour in an oven set to 480°F (250°C), using the top and bottom elements. Score the bread, place it in the pot, and put the lid on. Reduce the heat to 450°F (230°C). After 20 minutes, remove the lid and bake for another 20 minutes. Repeat the procedure for the second bread.

Long emmer bread

A rustic, oblong bread that's allowed to crack on its own. The dough should proof for a very long time so that the bread cracks nicely in the oven. If the bread cracks too much, it hasn't proofed long enough. I might add that I still misjudge the proofing for this type of bread. But if you manage to do it, it looks incredibly nice and the inside of the bread turns out just right.

Weight		Ingredients	Baker's percentage
total flour weight: 28 ¼ oz.	(800 g)	for 4 small breads	100 %
5 oz.	(140 g)	wholemeal emmer flour	17.5 %
23 ¼ oz.	(660 g)	sifted heritage wheat flour	82.5 %
21¾ oz.	(620 g)	water	77.5 %
5 ½ oz.	(160 g)	sourdough	20 %
¾ oz.	(18 g)	salt	2.5 %

12:00 Mix almost all the water, sourdough, and flour together in a bowl. Cover with a lid / kitchen towel.

12:30 Mix in the salt and the remaining water. Cover with a lid / kitchen towel.

13:00 Fold the dough over itself. Take one edge of the dough, pull it up, and fold it over itself. Rotate the bowl a quarter turn and repeat until you've folded all the dough. Cover with a lid / kitchen towel.

13:30 Fold the dough a second time.

14:00 Fold the dough a third time.

14:30 Fold the dough a fourth time.

16:30 Place a plastic bag over the bowl and place in the refrigerator.

Bake the next day. Place a baking steel or sheet pan in the middle of the oven. At the same time, place an oven-safe dish at the bottom of the oven. Preheat the oven to 480°F (250°C) for 1 hour, using the top and bottom elements.

Flour the counter thoroughly. Pour the dough out onto the counter and stretch it out a little so that you get a fairly even rectangle.

Flour the top of the dough thoroughly. Cut into four oblong strips / pieces of dough. Flour these further and roll them around gently with your hands so that the sides of the dough are also covered in flour.

Place the pieces of dough on a proofing cloth and pull up the cloth to create a small wall between each piece of dough.

Let the dough rest for 1–2 hours. The dough should start to get bubbles on the surface and look properly proofed.

Turn the dough out onto one or two sheets of baking paper, depending on the size of your oven. Slide into the oven (without scoring) using a peel. Pour ½–1 cups (100–200 ml) of boiling water into your baking dish and close the oven door. Reduce the heat to 450°F (230°C). Remove the baking dish with water after 20 minutes and bake for another 10–20 minutes. The speed of baking will vary depending on how many breads you put in the oven. Repeat the procedure if you split the dough between two sheets of baking paper.

Heritage baguette

For me, a baguette should be very airy and light. It should almost melt in your mouth. To make the baguettes as good as possible, I prefer to make and bake them on the same day.

Weight		Ingredients	Baker's percentage
total flour weight: 28 ¼ oz.	(800 g)	for 4 small baguettes	100 %
28 ¼ oz.	(800 g)	sifted heritage wheat flour	100 %
19 oz.	(540 g)	water	67.5 %
5 ½ oz.	(160 g)	sourdough	20 %
¾ oz.	(18 g)	salt	2.5 %

12:00 Mix almost all the water, sourdough, and flour together in a bowl. Cover with a lid / kitchen towel.

12:30 Mix in the salt and the remaining water. Cover with a lid / kitchen towel.

13:00 Fold the dough over itself. Take one edge of the dough, pull it up, and fold it over itself. Rotate the bowl a quarter turn and repeat until you've folded all the dough. Cover with a lid / kitchen towel.

13:30 Fold the dough a second time.

14:00 Fold the dough a third time.

14:30 Fold the dough a fourth time.

15:30 Divide the dough into four pieces. I prefer to make a slightly more oval preshape to prepare for the next step.

16:00 Final shape. Flour and turn over one of the pieces of dough using a dough scraper so that the sticky side is face up. Fold the bottom edge up so that it covers half. Fold the top down so that the seams meet. Then fold the bottom edge up again so that you double-fold the dough. Then roll with light, even pressure to get an oblong baguette. Apply a little extra pressure at the outer edges to get the characteristic taper. Place the dough seam-side up on a generously floured proofing cloth or kitchen towel. Pull up the cloth between each baguette so that you have a wall between them. Repeat with the other pieces of dough.

17:00 Place a baking steel or sheet pan in the middle of the oven. At the same time, place an oven-safe dish at the bottom of the oven. Preheat the oven to 480°F (250°C) for 1 hour, using the top and bottom elements.

18:00 Bake. Turn the dough out onto one or two sheets of baking paper, depending on the size of your oven. The seam should be face down. Flour, score, and slide into the oven using a peel. Pour ½–1 cups (100–200 ml) of boiling water into your baking dish and close the oven door. Reduce the heat to 450°F (230°C). Set a timer for 20 minutes. When the time is up, take out the baking dish with water. Continue baking for another 10–20 minutes. The speed will vary depending on how many breads you put in the oven. Repeat the procedure if you split the dough between two sheets of baking paper.

Spelt

A light bread with a slightly punchier flavor. In addition to the wholemeal spelt flour, I work with two different sifted flours when I make this bread. One of them is a stone-ground, sifted spelt flour that has a slightly darker color and deeper flavor. If you struggle to find stone-ground flour, use the spelt flour you can find ... It'll still be delicious. I shape the dough into a slightly more oblong shape and place in a proofing cloth.

Weight		Ingredients	Baker's percentage
total flour weight: 28 ¼ oz.	(800 g)	for 2 breads	100 %
2 ¾ oz.	(80 g)	wholemeal spelt flour	10 %
11 ¼ oz.	(320 g)	stone-ground sifted spelt flour	40 %
14 oz.	(400 g)	sifted heritage wheat flour	50 %
19 ¾ oz.	(560 g)	water	70 %
5 ½ oz.	(160 g)	sourdough	20 %
½ oz.	(16 g)	salt	2 %

12:00 Mix almost all the water, sourdough, and flour together in a bowl. Cover with a lid/kitchen towel.

12:30 Mix in the salt and the remaining water. Cover with a lid/kitchen towel.

13:00 Fold the dough over itself. Take one edge of the dough, pull it up, and fold it over itself. Rotate the bowl a quarter turn and repeat until you've folded all the dough. Cover with a lid/kitchen towel.

13:30 Fold the dough a second time.

14:00 Fold the dough a third time.

14:30 Fold the dough a fourth time.

16:30 Divide the dough in two. Preshape.

17:00 Final shape. Place a plastic bag over the baskets and place in the refrigerator.

Bake the next day. Preheat your baking sheet and the pot with the lid on for 1 hour in an oven set to 480°F (250°C), using the top and bottom elements. Score the bread, place it in the pot, and put the lid on. Reduce the heat to 450°F (230°C). After 20 minutes, remove the lid and bake for another 20 minutes. Repeat the procedure for the second bread.

Wilson's spelt

A baker named Wilson gave me the inspiration for this bread. It is lovely and coarse. To get it to crack itself, I prefer to make the dough and bake it the same day.

Weight		Ingredients	Baker's percentage
total flour weight: 28 ¼ oz.	(800 g)	for 2 breads	100 %
18 ⅓ oz.	(520 g)	wholemeal spelt flour	65 %
10 oz.	(280 g)	stone-ground sifted spelt flour	35 %
17 ⅔ oz.	(500 g)	water	62.5 %
7 oz.	(200 g)	sourdough	25 %
½ oz.	(16 g)	salt	2 %

12:00 Mix almost all the water, sourdough, and flour together in a bowl. Cover with a lid / kitchen towel.

12:30 Mix in the salt and the remaining water. Cover with a lid / kitchen towel.

13:00 Fold the dough over itself. Take one edge of the dough, pull it up, and fold it over itself. Rotate the bowl a quarter turn and repeat until you've folded all the dough. Cover with a lid / kitchen towel.

13:30 Fold the dough a second time.

16:30 Divide the dough in two. Preshape.

17:00 Final shape. This bread is best in a round proofing basket. The big difference from other breads is that I thoroughly flour the seam on the preshaped dough and then place it face down in the proofing basket, leaving the smooth side up.

Preheat your baking sheet for 1 hour in an oven set to 480°F (250°C), using the top and bottom elements.

18:00 Bake. Turn the bread out of the basket onto a sheet of baking paper so that the seam is now face up. Let the dough rest for about 10 minutes and allow it to open / crack slightly. Then place it in the pot with the baking paper (without scoring). Put the lid on and place in the oven. Lower the heat to 450°F (230°C). After 20 minutes, remove the lid and bake for another 20 minutes. Repeat the procedure for the second bread.

Crispbread

If you can make your own crispbread, it's a good idea to make double as it'll disappear before you know it. The dough is incredibly easy to make. The hard work comes in the rolling and baking.

Weight		Ingredients	Baker's percentage
total flour weight: 28 ¼ oz.	(800 g)	for about 15 crispbreads	100 %
21 ¼ oz.	(600 g)	wholemeal rye flour	75 %
7 oz.	(200 g)	wholemeal einkorn flour	25 %
18 ⅓ oz.	(520 g)	water	65 %
5 ½ oz.	(160 g)	sourdough	20 %
½ oz.	(16 g)	salt	2 %

12:00 Mix all the ingredients together in a bowl. Cover with a lid / kitchen towel.

12:30 If you're mixing by hand, it may be a good idea to work through the dough once more to make sure the dough is well mixed. If you use a food processor or dough mixer, you can skip this step. Cover with a lid / kitchen towel.

16:30 Place the dough bowl in the refrigerator until the next day.

Bake the next day. Preheat your baking steel or a sheet pan in the middle of an oven set to 400°F (200°C) for 1 hour, using the top and bottom elements.

Roll out the dough on a floured counter and divide into 15 (approximately 3 ½ ounces / 100 g) equal-sized balls. Flatten out one by one and roll out to the size of a frisbee. Use plenty of flour as the dough sticks easily.

Use a rolling pin and roll out on both sides. Punch out a ring in the middle with a small glass if you like.

Slide one crispbread into the oven at a time using a peel. If it's your first time doing this, it's easier if you use baking paper. Bake for about 10 minutes. Remember that things go quickly toward the end: Keep an eye on them so they don't burn.

Roll out the remaining crispbreads while the first one is baking and bake in batches … Imagine you're a crispbread factory. If you've rolled them thin enough, they'll break up easily and be nice and crispy. If they're too thick, the crispbreads will be a bit chewy and underdone. In this case, put them in the oven after you've finished baking and use the residual heat to harden them.

Breads with extra ingredients

Most of my recipes consist of a mixture of water, different types of flour, and sourdough. With these few ingredients, you can create an incredible number of different breads. But baking can be varied even more by mixing in some extra ingredients like fruit, nuts, and grains. It's really only your imagination that limits you.

In this chapter, you'll find bread that can be eaten every day, as well as breads for special occasions such as Christmas, crayfish parties, and Friday nights. These are recipes that often require a little more in terms of both effort and ingredients. But the results are all the more exciting, and the challenge of making the bread is even greater.

Durum & olives

A light, crispy bread with delicious black olives. I usually make this recipe as four smaller breads with slightly pointed ends and bake them on a baking steel. If the olives you're using are very large, you may want to cut them into smaller pieces.

Weight		Ingredients	Baker's percentage
total flour weight: 28 ¼ oz.	(800 g)	for 4 small breads	100 %
14 oz.	(400 g)	sifted durum flour	50 %
14 oz.	(400 g)	sifted heritage wheat flour	50 %
20 ½ oz.	(580 g)	water	72.5 %
5 ⅔ oz.	(160 g)	sourdough	20 %
½ oz.	(16 g)	salt	2 %
4 ¼ oz.	(120 g)	black olives, pitted	15 %

12:00 Mix almost all the water, sourdough, and flour together in a bowl. Cover with a lid/kitchen towel.

12:30 Mix in the salt and the remaining water. Cover with a lid/kitchen towel.

13:00 Fold the dough over itself. Take one edge of the dough, pull it up, and fold it over itself. Rotate the bowl a quarter turn and repeat until you've folded all the dough. Cover with a lid/kitchen towel.

13:30 Pour the olives into the dough bowl. Fold the dough over itself and in this way fold the olives into the dough. Cover with a lid/kitchen towel.

14:00 Fold the dough a third time.

14:30 Fold the dough a fourth time.

16:30 Preshape. Divide the dough in two.

17:00 Final shape. Place a plastic bag over the baskets and place in the refrigerator.

Bake the next day. Place a baking steel or sheet pan in the middle of the oven. At the same time, place an oven-safe dish at the bottom of the oven. Preheat the oven to 480°F (250°C) for 1 hour, using the top and bottom elements.

Take one of the proofing baskets out of the refrigerator. Roll out the dough onto a sheet of baking paper. Divide the dough lengthwise with a dough scraper. Flour the cut surface so that it's "closed" by the flour and then turn the dough so that the floured cut is face down on the sheet of baking paper. Press the ends a little to make them pointy. Flour, score, and slide into the oven using a peel. Pour ½–1 cups (100–200 ml) of boiling water into your baking dish and close the oven door. Reduce the oven temperature to 450°F (230°C). Set a timer for 20 minutes. When the time is up, take out the baking dish with water. Bake the bread for about another 10 minutes. Repeat the procedure for the second piece of dough.

Fennel & figs

I find this particular bread absolutely delicious when toasted with butter and generously topped with tasty brie. Add a few figs on the side and you have a rich mix that'll delight your taste buds.

Weight	Ingredients	Baker's percentage
total flour weight: 28 ¼ oz. (800 g)	for 2 breads	100 %
2 ¾ oz. (80 g)	wholemeal landrace rye flour	10 %
25 ⅓ oz. (720 g)	bread flour	90 %
21 ¼ oz. (600 g)	water	75 %
5 ⅔ oz. (160 g)	sourdough	20 %
½ oz. (16 g)	salt	2 %
1 ⅓ oz. (40 g)	honey	5 %
4 ¼ oz. (120 g)	dried figs	15 %
3 g	fennel seeds	0.375 %

11:00 Cut each fig into 4–6 pieces. Don't forget to cut off and discard the hard little top. Place the figs in a small bowl and pour just enough water (from the total amount of water in the recipe) to cover them. You usually need about the same amount of water by weight as dried fruit. Mortar the fennel seeds.

12:00 Mix the remaining water, sourdough, and flour in a bowl. Cover with a lid/kitchen towel.

12:30 Mix in the salt, fennel seeds, honey, figs, and the water they were in. Work the dough together so that everything is mixed. Cover with a lid/kitchen towel.

13:00 Fold the dough over itself. Take one edge of the dough, pull it up, and fold it over itself. Rotate the bowl a quarter turn and repeat until you've folded all the dough. Cover with a lid/kitchen towel.

13:30 Fold the dough a second time.

14:00 Fold the dough a third time.

14:30 Fold the dough a fourth time.

16:30 Divide the dough in two. Preshape.

17:00 Final shape. Place a plastic bag over the baskets and place in the refrigerator.

Bake the next day. Preheat your baking sheet and the pot with the lid on for 1 hour in an oven set to 480°F (250°C), using the top and bottom elements. Score the bread, place it in the pot, and put the lid on. Reduce the heat to 450°F (230°C). After 20 minutes, remove the lid and bake for another 20 minutes. Repeat the procedure for the second bread.

Fruit & nuts

Fruit and nuts—bread with extra everything. My mom is incredibly fond of this type of bread, so I bake it regularly.

Weight	Ingredients	Baker's percentage
total flour weight: 28 ¼ oz. (800 g)	for 2 breads	100 %
3 ½ oz. (100 g)	wholemeal einkorn flour	12.5 %
24 ¾ oz. (720 g)	bread flour	90 %
21 ¾ oz. (620 g)	water	77.5 %
5 ½ oz. (160 g)	sourdough	20 %
⅔ oz. (18 g)	salt	2.25 %
1 ⅓ oz. (40 g)	dried apricots	5 %
1 ⅓ oz. (40 g)	dried figs	5 %
1 ⅓ oz. (40 g)	raisins	5 %
1 ⅓ oz. (40 g)	walnuts	5 %
1 ⅓ oz. (40 g)	hazelnuts	5 %

11:00 Spread the hazelnuts on one half of a sheet pan and the walnuts on the other side. Toast in the oven at 350°F (180°C) for about 10 minutes. Place the hazelnuts in a towel immediately after roasting and massage the lot to remove any excess shells. Chop the apricots and figs into small pieces. Place all the fruit, including the raisins, in a small bowl and pour just enough water (from the total amount of water in the recipe) to cover all the fruit. You usually need about the same amount of water by weight as dried fruit. Coarsely chop the walnuts (I leave the hazelnuts whole).

12:00 Mix the remaining water, sourdough, and flour in a bowl. Cover with a lid/kitchen towel.

12:30 Mix in the salt and the dried fruit, as well as the water the fruit was soaked in. Cover with a lid/kitchen towel.

13:00 Fold the dough over itself. Take one edge of the dough, pull it up, and fold it over itself. Rotate the bowl a quarter turn and repeat until you've folded all the dough. Cover with a lid/kitchen towel.

13:30 Pour the nuts into the dough bowl. Fold the dough over itself and in this way fold the nuts into the dough. Cover with a lid/kitchen towel.

14:00 Fold the dough a third time.

14:30 Fold the dough a fourth time.

16:30 Divide the dough in two. Preshape.

17:00 Final shape. Place a plastic bag over the baskets and place in the refrigerator.

Bake the next day. Preheat your baking sheet and the pot with the lid on for 1 hour in an oven set to 480°F (250°C), using the top and bottom elements. Score the bread, place it in the pot, and put the lid on. Reduce the heat to 450°F (230°C). After 20 minutes, remove the lid and bake for another 20 minutes. Repeat the procedure for the second bread.

Lemon & poppy seed

A bread that turns out incredibly fresh and delicious. It goes phenomenally well at a crayfish party and other celebrations.

Weight		Ingredients	Baker's percentage
total flour weight: 28 ¼ oz.	(800 g)	for 2 breads	100 %
2 ¾ oz.	(80 g)	wholemeal heritage wheat flour	10 %
25 ⅓ oz.	(720 g)	bread flour	90 %
21 ¼ oz.	(600 g)	water	75 %
5 ½ oz.	(160 g)	sourdough	20 %
½ oz.	(16 g)	salt	2 %
		+ zest from 1 lemon	
		+ poppy seeds	

12:00 Mix almost all the water, sourdough, and flour together in a bowl. Cover with a lid / kitchen towel.

12:30 Mix in the salt, lemon zest, and the remaining water. Cover with a lid / kitchen towel.

13:00 Fold the dough over itself. Take one edge of the dough, pull it up, and fold it over itself. Rotate the bowl a quarter turn and repeat until you've folded all the dough. Cover with a lid / kitchen towel.

13:30 Fold the dough a second time.

14:00 Fold the dough a third time.

14:30 Fold the dough a fourth time.

16:30 Divide the dough in two. Preshape.

17:00 Final shape. Prepare a plate or tray with the poppy seeds. After the final shape, spray or brush the dough with water and then take it out and roll it in the seeds. Then place in proofing baskets as usual with the seam face up. Place a plastic bag over the baskets and place in the refrigerator.

Bake the next day. Preheat your baking sheet and the pot with the lid on for 1 hour in an oven set to 480°F (250°C), using the top and bottom elements. Score the bread, place it in the pot, and put the lid on. Reduce the heat to 450°F (230°C). After 20 minutes, remove the lid and bake for another 20 minutes. Repeat the procedure for the second bread.

Västerbotten & dill

A flavorful bread that goes well with seafood or fish soup, for example. Its crust and interior wonderfully absorb and complement the flavors of the food. Västerbotten cheese is a mature hard cheese from Sweden, known for its unique, robust flavor. If you can't find it, substitute with another hard cheese like Parmesan or Cheddar for similar texture and savory depth.

Weight		Ingredients	Baker's percentage
total flour weight: 28 ¼ oz.	(800 g)	for 2 breads	100 %
2 ¾ oz.	(80 g)	wholemeal heritage wheat flour	10 %
25 ⅓ oz.	(720 g)	bread flour	90 %
21 ¼ oz.	(600 g)	water	75 %
5 ½ oz.	(160 g)	sourdough	20 %
½ oz.	(16 g)	salt	2 %
4 ¼ oz.	(120 g)	Västerbotten cheese	15 %
2 g		dill seeds	0.25 %
¾ oz.	(20 g)	fresh dill	2.5 %
		+ zest from 1 lemon	

11:00 Mortar the dill seeds, chop the dill, and dice the cheese into ½-inch (1 cm) sized cubes.

12:00 Mix almost all the water, sourdough, and flour together in a bowl. Cover with a lid / kitchen towel.

12:30 Mix in the salt, fresh dill, dill seeds, and the remaining water. Cover with a lid / kitchen towel.

13:00 Fold the dough for the first time. Take one edge of the dough, pull it up, and fold it over itself. Rotate the bowl a quarter turn and repeat the process until you've folded the entire dough over itself. Cover with a lid / kitchen towel.

13:30 Pour the cheese into the dough bowl. Fold the dough over itself and in this way fold the cheese into the dough. Cover with a lid / kitchen towel.

14:00 Fold the dough a third time.

14:30 Fold the dough a fourth time.

16:30 Divide the dough in two. Preshape.

17:00 Final shape. Place a plastic bag over the baskets and place in the refrigerator.

Bake the next day. Preheat your baking sheet and the pot with the lid on for 1 hour in an oven set to 480°F (250°C), using the top and bottom elements. Score the bread, place it in the pot, and put the lid on. Reduce the heat to 450°F (230°C). After 20 minutes, remove the lid and bake for another 20 minutes. Repeat the procedure for the second bread.

Blueberry & pistachio

An exciting and delicious bread that blends the sweetness of the blueberries with the saltiness of the nuts. Its very special character is revealed with every slice.

Weight		Ingredients	Baker's percentage
total flour weight: 28 ¼ oz.	(800 g)	for 2 breads	100 %
2 ¾ oz.	(80 g)	wholemeal heritage wheat flour	10 %
25 ⅓ oz.	(720 g)	bread flour	90 %
21 ¼ oz.	(600 g)	water	75 %
5 ½ oz.	(160 g)	sourdough	20 %
½ oz.	(16 g)	salt	2 %
3 ½ oz.	(100 g)	fresh blueberries	12.5 %
3 ½ oz.	(100 g)	shelled, salted pistachios	12.5 %

12:00 Mix almost all the water, sourdough, and flour together in a bowl. Cover with a lid / kitchen towel.

12:30 Mix in the salt and the remaining water. Cover with a lid / kitchen towel.

13:00 Fold the dough over itself. Take one edge of the dough, pull it up, and fold it over itself. Rotate the bowl a quarter turn and repeat until you've folded all the dough. Cover with a lid / kitchen towel.

13:30 Pour the blueberries and nuts into the dough bowl. Fold the dough over itself and in this way fold everything into the dough. Cover with a lid / kitchen towel.

14:00 Fold the dough a third time.

14:30 Fold the dough a fourth time.

16:30 Divide the dough in two. Preshape.

17:00 Final shape. Place a plastic bag over the baskets and place in the refrigerator.

Bake the next day. Preheat your baking sheet and the pot with the lid on for 1 hour in an oven set to 480°F (250°C), using the top and bottom elements. Score the bread, place it in the pot, and put the lid on. Reduce the heat to 450°F (230°C). After 20 minutes, remove the lid and bake for another 20 minutes. Repeat the procedure for the second bread.

Wort bread with stout

A wort bread that uses stout as the dough liquid gives a lovely malty flavor. I recommend using a stout that is dark and strong in both color and alcohol content. The alcohol evaporates during baking. The whole idea is that it should be a dark liquid to give some color and character.

Weight		Ingredients	Baker's percentage
total flour weight: 28 ¼ oz.	(800 g)	for 2 breads	100 %
5 ⅔ oz.	(160 g)	wholemeal rye flour	20 %
22 ½ oz.	(640 g)	bread flour	80 %
11 ¼ oz.	(320 g)	dark stout	40 %
10 oz.	(280 g)	low-alcohol malt ale/dark beer	35 %
8 ½ oz.	(240 g)	sourdough	30 %
½ oz.	(16 g)	salt	2 %
2 ¾ oz.	(80 g)	raw syrup or dark syrup	10 %
3 ½ oz.	(100 g)	raisins	12.5 %
¼ oz.	(8 g)	spices	1 %
1 g		ground star anise	
0.5 g		ground cloves	
1 g		ground cardamom	
1.5 g		bitter orange	
2 g		Ceylon cinnamon	
2 g		ground ginger	

11:00 Place the raisins in a small bowl and pour just enough of the low-alcohol drink or beer (from the total amount of liquid in the recipe) to cover them. It usually requires about the same amount of liquid by weight as dried fruit.

12:00 Mix together the stout and remaining low-alcohol drink or beer, sourdough, and flour in a bowl. Cover with a lid/kitchen towel.

12:30 Mortar the spices. Mix the salt, spices, syrup, and the soaked raisins, including the liquid they're in, into the dough. Cover with a lid/kitchen towel.

13:00 Fold the dough over itself. Take one edge of the dough, pull it up, and fold it over itself. Rotate the bowl a quarter turn and repeat until you've folded all the dough. Cover with a lid/kitchen towel.

13:30 Fold the dough a second time.

14:00 Fold the dough a third time.

14:30 Fold the dough a fourth time.

17:30 Divide the dough in two. Preshape.

18:00 Final shape. Place the baskets in the refrigerator if the dough looks airy and risen (place a plastic bag over the baskets). If not, let the doughs proof in their baskets for another 1 or 2 hours before placing them in the refrigerator.

Bake the next day. Preheat your baking sheet and the pot with the lid on for 1 hour in an oven set to 480°F (250°C), using the top and bottom elements. Score the bread, place it in the pot, and put the lid on. Reduce the heat to 450°F (230°C). After 20 minutes, remove the lid and bake for another 20 minutes. Repeat the procedure for the second bread.

Caution! Because the bread contains a lot of sugar, it easily burns on the bottom if baked too hot.

Holiday

A festive bread for holidays such as Christmas if you don't like wort bread. The bread tastes and smells absolutely wonderful.

Weight		Ingredients	Baker's percentage
total flour weight: 28 ¼ oz.	(800 g)	for 2 breads	100 %
2 ¾ oz.	(80 g)	graham flour	10 %
25 ⅓ oz.	(720 g)	bread flour	90 %
21 ¼ oz.	(600 g)	water	75 %
7 oz.	(200 g)	sourdough	25 %
½ oz.	(16 g)	salt	2 %
2 oz.	(60 g)	dried sour cherries	7.5 %
2 oz.	(60 g)	raisins	7.5 %
2 ¾ oz.	(80 g)	pecan nuts	10 %
2 ¾ oz.	(80 g)	maple syrup	10 %
2 g		Ceylon cinnamon	0.25 %
2 g		ground ginger	0.25 %
		+ zest from 1 orange	

11:00 Place the cherries and raisins in a bowl and pour just enough water (from the total amount of water in the recipe) to cover them. You usually need about the same amount of water by weight as dried fruit.

12:00 Mix the remaining water, sourdough, and flour in a bowl. The dough will be quite dry when first mixed. If necessary, take the dough out and knead it through. Cover with a lid / kitchen towel.

12:30 Mix in the salt, spices, maple syrup, orange zest, soaked fruit, and the water the fruit was in. There's quite a lot of liquid going into the dough so you'll need to work for a little while. Cover with a lid / kitchen towel.

13:00 Fold the dough over itself. Take one edge of the dough, pull it up, and fold it over itself. Rotate the bowl a quarter turn and repeat until you've folded all the dough. Cover with a lid / kitchen towel.

13:30 Pour the nuts into the dough. Fold the dough over itself and fold the nuts into the dough in this way. Cover with a lid / kitchen towel.

14:00 Fold the dough a third time.

14:30 Fold the dough a fourth time.

17:30 Divide the dough in two. Preshape.

18:00 Final shape. Place the baskets in the refrigerator if the dough looks airy and risen (place a plastic bag over the baskets). If not, let the dough proof in their baskets for another 1–2 hours before placing them in the refrigerator. Sweetened dough generally tends to be a bit slow-proofing.

Bake the next day. Preheat your baking sheet and the pot with the lid on for 1 hour in an oven set to 480°F (250°C), using the top and bottom elements. Score the bread, place it in the pot, and put the lid on. Reduce the heat to 450°F (230°C). After 20 minutes, remove the lid and bake for another 20 minutes. Repeat the procedure for the second bread.

Lingonberry & juniper

This bread has a lovely forest feel and aroma. Take the opportunity to make this bread during the late summer when lingonberries are in season. You can also use thawed frozen lingonberries, but you have to be a little more careful as they break more easily.

Weight		Ingredients	Baker's percentage
total flour weight: 28 ¼ oz.	(800 g)	for 2 breads	100 %
5 ⅔ oz.	(160 g)	wholemeal landrace rye flour	20 %
5 ⅔ oz.	(160 g)	wholemeal rye flour	20 %
17 oz.	(480 g)	sifted heritage wheat flour	60 %
19 ¾ oz.	(560 g)	water	70 %
7 oz.	(200 g)	sourdough	25 %
⅔ oz.	(18 g)	salt	2.25 %
1 ¾ oz.	(50 g)	rye bran	6.25 %
+ 3 ½ oz.	(100 g)	water (for scalding)	
5 ⅔ oz.	(160 g)	lingonberries	20 %
3 g		juniper (mortared spice)	0.375 %
2 ¾ oz.	(80 g)	honey	10 %

Toast the rye the night before you're going to make the dough. Spread out on a sheet pan and place in the oven for about 15 minutes at 350°F (175°C). Let the rye bran start to smoke and take on a nice color and aroma. Pour the rye bran into a bowl and then pour boiling water over it. Stir a little, put a lid on, and leave until the next day.

12:00 Mix all the water, sourdough, and flour together in a bowl. Cover with a lid / kitchen towel.

12:30 Mix in the salt, honey, crushed juniper berries, and rye bran. Cover with a lid / kitchen towel.

13:00 Fold the dough over itself. Take one edge of the dough, pull it up, and fold it over itself. Rotate the bowl a quarter turn and repeat until you've folded all the dough. Cover with a lid / kitchen towel.

13:30 Pour in the lingonberries. Fold the dough over itself and in this way fold the lingonberries into the dough. Cover with a lid / kitchen towel.

14:00 Fold the dough a third time.

14:30 Fold the dough a fourth time.

16:30 Divide the dough in two. Preshape.

17:00 Flour the pieces of dough generously and turn them into their own basket. Place a plastic bag over the baskets and place in the refrigerator.

Bake the next day. Preheat your baking sheet and the pot with the lid on for 1 hour in an oven set to 480°F (250°C), using the top and bottom elements. Score the bread, place it in the pot, and put the lid on. Reduce the heat to 450°F (230°C). After 20 minutes, remove the lid and bake for another 20 minutes. Repeat the procedure for the second bread.

Rye pie

There is a bread that originates in the Alps called tourte de seigle. *Roughly translated it means "rye pie," which I thought sounded fun. As with all breads, there are different varieties, with and without spices and the like. This is my interpretation.*

Weight	Ingredients	Baker's percentage
total flour weight: 28 ¼ oz. (800 g)	for 2 breads	100 %
28 ¼ oz. (800 g)	landrace rye flour	100 %
21¼ oz. (600 g)	water	75 %
11¼ oz. (320 g)	sourdough	40 %
⅔ oz. (18 g)	salt	2.25 %
4 ¼ oz. (120 g)	honey	15 %
1⅓ oz. (40 g)	malt syrup / liquid wort	5 %
1 g	crushed / mortared fennel seeds	0.125 %
1 g	crushed / mortared anise	0.125 %
2 g	crushed / mortared caraway seeds	0.25 %

12:00 Mix all the ingredients together in the dough bowl and work together until the dough feels well-mixed and smooth. Cover with a lid / kitchen towel.

12:30 If you're mixing by hand, it may be a good idea to work through the dough once more with your hands to make sure the dough is well mixed. If you use a dough mixer, you can skip this step.

13:30 Roll out the dough on the counter and divide into two. With wet hands, form two balls. Then roll the balls in plenty of rye flour and place each into its own round proofing basket. Cover with a kitchen towel. Let them proof until they've grown and large cracks have formed in the surface of the dough.

17:00 Preheat your baking sheet for 1 hour in an oven set to 480°F (250°C), using the top and bottom elements.

18:00 Place one of the pieces of dough onto a sheet of baking paper. Let the dough sit for about 10 minutes until new cracks form on the surface (because this was the underside, which usually becomes smooth when sitting in the basket). Place the baking paper and dough in the pot and put the lid on. Bake. Reduce the heat to 410°F (210°C). After 20 minutes, remove the lid and bake for another 20–25 minutes. Repeat the procedure for the second bread.

Cover the breads with plastic wrap once they've cooled so the crust softens. The breads need to sit and are best eaten the next morning.

Potato & thyme

A delicious, hearty bread for soup.

Weight		Ingredients	Baker's percentage
total flour weight: 28 ¼ oz.	(800 g)	for 2 breads	100 %
1⅓ oz.	(40 g)	wholemeal rye flour	5 %
1⅓ oz.	(40 g)	graham flour	5 %
25 ⅓ oz.	(720 g)	bread flour	90 %
19 ¾ oz.	(560 g)	water	70 %
5 ½ oz.	(160 g)	sourdough	20 %
¾ oz.	(20 g)	salt	2.5 %
14 oz.	(400 g)	boiled, peeled, mashed potatoes	50 %
2 g		thyme (dried herb)	0.25 %
		+ raw potatoes, fresh thyme, salt flakes, and black pepper	

12:00 Mix almost all the water, sourdough, and flour together in a bowl. Cover with a lid / kitchen towel.

12:30 Mix in the salt, mashed potatoes, thyme, and remaining water. Cover with a lid / kitchen towel.

13:00 Fold the dough over itself. Take one edge of the dough, pull it up, and fold it over itself. Rotate the bowl a quarter turn and repeat until you've folded all the dough. Cover with a lid / kitchen towel.

13:30 Fold the dough a second time.

14:00 Fold the dough a third time.

14:30 Fold the dough a fourth time.

16:30 Divide the dough in two. Preshape.

17:00 Flour the dough and two sheets of baking paper. Then transfer the pieces of dough to separate sheets of baking paper. Stretch the pieces of dough out into large rectangles. Lightly flour them, cover with a kitchen towel, and let them rise nicely.

17:30 Place a baking steel or sheet pan in the middle of the oven. At the same time, place an oven-safe dish at the bottom of the oven. Preheat the oven to 480°F (250°C) for 1 hour, using the top and bottom elements.

18:30 When the dough looks big and fluffy, it's time to bake.

Slice raw potatoes thinly and spread over the dough. Sprinkle with fresh thyme, salt flakes, and a few grinds of black pepper. Use a dough scraper or pizza slicer and cut across the entire dough all the way down so you get a square pattern.

Slide one of the pieces of dough into the oven using a peel. Pour ½–1 cup (100–200 ml) of boiling water into the baking dish and close the oven door. Remove the baking dish with water after 20 minutes and bake for another 5–10 minutes. Repeat the procedure for the next piece of dough.

When the bread is ready, it will have baked back together in the oven. Break the bread apart immediately and place in a basket or on a cutting board. Place on the dining table and let everyone break off their own chunks.

Cheddar & jalapeno

A delicious and decorative bread with a little bite.

Weight		Ingredients	Baker's percentage
total flour weight: 28 ¼ oz.	(800 g)	for 2 breads	100 %
1⅓ oz.	(40 g)	wholemeal rye flour	5 %
1⅓ oz.	(40 g)	graham flour	5 %
25 ⅓ oz.	(720 g)	bread flour	90 %
19 ¾ oz.	(560 g)	water	70 %
5 ½ oz.	(160 g)	sourdough	20 %
¾ oz.	(20 g)	salt	2.5 %
2 ¾ oz.	(80 g)	pickled, sliced jalapeño	10 %
4 ¼ oz.	(120 g)	diced cheddar cheese	15 %

12:00 Mix almost all the water, sourdough, and flour together in a bowl. Cover with a lid/kitchen towel.

12:30 Mix in the salt and the remaining water. Cover with a lid/kitchen towel.

13:00 Fold the dough over itself. Take one edge of the dough, pull it up, and fold it over itself. Rotate the bowl a quarter turn and repeat until you've folded all the dough. Cover with a lid/kitchen towel.

13:30 Pour the cheese and jalapeños into the dough bowl. Fold the dough over itself and in this way fold everything into the dough. Cover with a lid/kitchen towel.

14:00 Fold the dough a third time.

14:30 Fold the dough a fourth time.

16:30 Divide the dough in two. Preshape.

17:00 Flour the dough and two sheets of baking paper. Then transfer the pieces of dough to separate sheets of baking paper. Make a hole in the middle of the pieces of dough. Your elbow or a shot glass works well. Then stretch the pieces of dough out a little into nice, even round shapes. Flour them, cover with a kitchen towel, and let them rise nicely.

Bake. Place a baking steel or sheet pan in the middle of the oven. At the same time, place an oven-safe dish at the bottom of the oven. Preheat the oven to 480°F (250°C) for 1 hour, using the top and bottom elements.

18:00 When the dough looks big and fluffy, it's time to bake. Slide one of the pieces of dough into the oven using a peel. Pour ½–1 cups (100–200 ml) of boiling water into your baking dish and close the oven door. Lower the heat to 450°F (230°C). Set a timer for 20 minutes. When the time is up, take out the baking dish with water. Now set the timer for 10 minutes and check every time it rings. It usually takes about 30–40 minutes in total to bake. Let the baking steel and baking dish reheat for about 20 minutes before baking the next bread.

Ciabatta

A wonderfully crispy and light bread.

Weight		Ingredients	Baker's percentage
total flour weight: 28 ¼ oz. (800 g)		for about 6 breads	100 %
28 ¼ oz.	(800 g)	bread flour	100 %
24 oz.	(680 g)	water	85 %
7 oz.	(200 g)	sourdough	25 %
¾ oz.	(20 g)	salt	2.5 %
¾ oz.	(20 g)	olive oil	2.5 %

12:00 Mix together almost all the water (start with 21 ¼ ounces/600 g), sourdough, and flour in a bowl. Cover with a lid/kitchen towel.

12:30 Mix in the salt and half of the remaining water (1 ⅓ ounces/40 g). Cover with a lid/kitchen towel.

13:00 Add the last of the water and fold the dough over itself. Take one edge of the dough, pull it up, and fold it over itself. Rotate the bowl a quarter turn and repeat until you've folded all the dough. Cover with a lid/kitchen towel.

13:30 Pour the olive oil into the dough and work it in by folding the dough. All the oil should be mixed into the dough when the last fold is done. Cover with a lid/kitchen towel.

14:00 Fold the dough a third time.

14:30 Fold the dough a fourth time.

16:30 Place the entire dough bowl in the refrigerator until the next day.

Bake the next day. Place a baking steel or sheet pan in the middle of the oven. At the same time, place an oven-safe dish at the bottom of the oven. Preheat the oven to 480°F (250°C) for 1 hour, using the top and bottom elements.

Flour the counter thoroughly. Pour all the dough onto the floured counter. Flour the top quite generously. Stretch the dough out so that you get a fairly oblong rectangular shape. The idea is that you should get six even rectangles from the dough. I usually start by dividing the entire dough in half, lengthwise. Then I cut out three approximately equal-sized pieces from each "strip." Place the dough pieces on a generously floured proofing cloth and pull the sheet up between the pieces so that they have an edge to rest against. Let them sit for at least 1 hour, preferably 2, until they become puffy and gas bubbles appear in the surface of the dough.

When it's time to bake, use a peel and your other hand to flip the dough pieces over so they end up upside down on a sheet of baking paper.

I usually bake three or four breads at a time. Slide the sheet of baking paper and the dough into the oven (without scoring) using a peel. Pour ½–1 cups (100–200 ml) of boiling water into your baking dish and close the oven door.

Set a timer for 15 minutes and check the bread when the time is up. It usually takes 15–20 minutes in total to bake.

Repeat the procedure with the other sheet of baking paper.

Pizza dough

Pizza baked at home in the oven benefits from a little olive oil in the dough. The dough stays a little softer and takes on a nice color in the oven faster. If you use a pizza oven, you can skip the oil in the dough.

Weight		Ingredients	Baker's percentage
total flour weight: 28 ¼ oz.	(800 g)	for about 6 pizzas	100 %
28 ¼ oz.	(800 g)	bread flour	100 %
18 ⅓ oz.	(520 g)	water	65 %
7 oz.	(200 g)	sourdough	25 %
¾ oz.	(20 g)	salt	2.5 %
½ oz.	(16 g)	olive oil	2 %

12:00 Mix the water, sourdough, and flour in a bowl. Cover with a lid / kitchen towel.

12:30 Mix in the salt. Cover with a lid / kitchen towel.

13:00 Fold the dough over itself. Take one edge of the dough, pull it up, and fold it over itself. Rotate the bowl a quarter turn and repeat until you've folded all the dough. Cover with a lid / kitchen towel.

13:30 Pour the olive oil into the dough and work it in by folding the dough. All the oil should be mixed into the dough when the last fold is done. Cover with a lid / kitchen towel.

14:00 Fold the dough a third time.

14:30 Fold the dough a fourth time.

15:00 Pour the dough out onto the counter and divide it into six equal pieces. Preshape. Place the dough balls in individual small bowls or place tightly together so that they support each other in a suitable baking dish. Cover with plastic.

16:30 Place in the refrigerator until the next day.

Bake the next day. Place your baking steel almost at the top of the oven. Preheat the oven to 480°F (250°C) for 1 hour, using the top and bottom elements.

Use plenty of flour when you turn out the dough onto the counter to start shaping the pizzas. Flatten the dough with your hands. If the dough is stiff, let it rest for a few minutes until it "relaxes." Once you've flattened the dough to ¾ of the desired size, transfer the dough to a sheet of baking paper and add any toppings you want. Then grab the edges of the dough and pull them out a little to make the finished pizza a little larger. The topping usually acts as a good weight and lubricant to achieve the final nice shape of the pizza.

When you put the pizza in the oven, turn on the grill function to give it a heat boost. In my home oven, it usually takes about 5 minutes to bake a pizza.

Focaccia

Focaccia is the ultimate snack bread. It's super delicious on its own, but you can also dip it, eat it as finger food, or make hearty sandwiches out of it. The pan I use is 9½ × 9½ inches (24 × 24 cm) and this dough fills it perfectly. If you have a larger pan, you can increase the recipe.

Weight	Ingredients	Baker's percentage
total flour weight: 14 oz. (400 g)	for 1 focaccia	100 %
10½ oz. (300 g)	bread flour	75 %
3½ oz. (100 g)	sifted durum flour	25 %
11¼ oz. (320 g)	water	80 %
4¼ oz. (120 g)	sourdough	30 %
⅓ oz. (11 g)	salt	2.75 %
⅓ oz. (10 g)	olive oil	2.5 %
	+ additional olive oil for garnishing	
	+ fresh rosemary and salt flakes	
	+ optional olives, cherry tomatoes, sun-dried tomatoes, and feta cheese	

12:00 Mix together almost all the water (10 ounces/280 g), sourdough, and flour in a bowl. Cover with a lid/kitchen towel.

12:30 Mix in the salt and half (¾ ounces/20 g) of the remaining water. Cover with a lid/kitchen towel.

13:00 Add the last of the water and fold the dough over itself. Take one edge of the dough, pull it up, and fold it over itself. Rotate the bowl a quarter turn and repeat until you've folded all the dough. Cover with a lid/kitchen towel.

13:30 Pour the olive oil into the dough and work it in by folding the dough. All the oil should be mixed into the dough when the last fold is done. Cover with a lid/kitchen towel.

14:00 Fold the dough a third time.

14:30 Fold the dough a fourth time.

15:00 Carefully pour the dough into an oiled ovenproof dish and cover it with plastic wrap.

18:00 Before baking, preheat the oven to 480°F (250°C) for 1 hour, using the top and bottom elements.

19:00 Once the dough looks puffy, pour over a little more olive oil and spread it out with your fingers so that the dough is covered. Then press your fingers into the dough so that the surface becomes bumpy and uneven. Sprinkle with salt flakes and fresh rosemary. If you want more ingredients, you can stuff tomatoes, olives, and other goodies into the small cavities.

Place in the middle of the oven and bake for about 25 minutes. When the bread is golden, remove it from the oven and let it cool for a while in the pan. Remove the bread and place it on a cutting board. Cut into squares and enjoy.

A different kind of pizza

This is reminiscent of Roman-style pizza, something my wife and I ate a lot when we were in Rome. These pizzas are often made large and rectangular and then cut into smaller square pieces. There are often lots of toppings to choose from, with everything from white pizzas that are sparsely topped to more decadent varieties. The pizza base is a little thicker, oilier, and also crispier than the previous pizza dough. It's the perfect food for a party or social gathering. I use focaccia dough for this recipe.

Weight		Ingredients	Baker's percentage
total flour weight: 14 oz.	(400 g)	for 1 sheet pan-sized pizza	100 %
10 ½ oz.	(300 g)	bread flour	75 %
3 ½ oz.	(100 g)	sifted durum flour	25 %
11 ¼ oz.	(320 g)	water	80 %
4 ¼ oz.	(120 g)	sourdough	30 %
⅓ oz.	(11 g)	salt	2.75 %
⅓ oz.	(10 g)	olive oil	2.5 %
		+ additional olive oil for garnishing	

12:00 Mix together almost all the water (10 ounces/280 g), sourdough, and flour in a bowl. Cover with a lid/kitchen towel.

12:30 Mix in the salt and half (¾ ounces/20 g) of the remaining water. Cover with a lid/kitchen towel.

13:00 Add the last of the water and fold the dough over itself. Take one edge of the dough, pull it up, and fold it over itself. Rotate the bowl a quarter turn and repeat until you've folded all the dough. Cover with a lid/kitchen towel.

13:30 Pour the olive oil into the dough and work it in by folding the dough. All the oil should be mixed into the dough when the last fold is done. Cover with a kitchen towel.

14:00 Fold the dough a third time.

14:30 Fold the dough a fourth time.

16:30 Wrap in plastic and place in the refrigerator until the next day.

Bake the next day. Before baking, preheat your baking steel or a sheet pan in the middle of the oven set to 400°F (250°C) for 1 hour, using the top and bottom elements.

Prepare a sheet of baking paper and oil it generously with olive oil. Roll out the dough onto the sheet of baking paper. Oil the top of the dough to make it easier to work with. Pull the dough out until it starts to stretch. Pause for 5–10 minutes so that it can "relax" before pulling it out further. Pause and repeat if necessary. Press your fingertips into the dough, as you would with a focaccia, to press the dough out further.

Top the pizzas or simply prebake with olive oil, crème fraiche, or tomato sauce and then top further once the pizza is out of the oven with things like roasted vegetables, cured meats, burrata, or anything else you find tasty on a pizza.

Slide into the middle of the oven and bake for 15–20 minutes, until the pizza is nicely browned. Cut into squares, add any extra tasty toppings, and enjoy immediately.

Porridge, groats & whole grains

Making porridge from different grains and mixing it into the dough is fantastic. It adds a creaminess and a lovely flavor to the bread. Although most people are familiar with oatmeal, the selection of different porridges is much larger and you can find a lot of different varieties.

Even whole, crushed, or cut grains are good in bread. I prefer to boil the grains and blanch the groats the day before I make the dough so that they have enough time to absorb the water, get the right consistency, and cool down. If you have leftover porridge from breakfast, bread is definitely a great way to use it.

These breads are usually healthy but also, most importantly, incredibly tasty!

Oat porridge bread

Oat porridge bread, or oatmeal bread, has a nice ring to it, doesn't it? Oatmeal goes incredibly well in bread.

Weight		Ingredients	Baker's percentage
total flour weight: 28 ¼ oz.	(800 g)	for 2 breads	100 %
4 ¼ oz.	(120 g)	wholemeal heritage wheat flour	15 %
12 oz.	(340 g)	bread flour	42.5 %
12 oz.	(340 g)	sifted heritage wheat flour	42.5 %
19 ¾ oz.	(560 g)	water	70 %
5 ½ oz.	(160 g)	sourdough	20 %
¾ oz.	(20 g)	salt	2.5 %
4 ¼ oz.	(120 g)	oatmeal	15 %
8 ½ oz.	(240 g)	water (for oatmeal)	30 %
		+ extra oatmeal to cover the bread with	

The night before you're going to make the dough, boil 8 ½ ounces (240 g) of water and blanch 4 ¼ ounces (120 g) of oatmeal. Put the lid on and let it stand until the next day.

12:00 Mix almost all the water, sourdough, and flour together in a bowl. Cover with a lid / kitchen towel.

12:30 Mix in the salt, porridge, and remaining water. Cover with a lid / kitchen towel.

13:00 Fold the dough over itself. Take one edge of the dough, pull it up, and fold it over itself. Rotate the bowl a quarter turn and repeat until you've folded all the dough. Cover with a lid / kitchen towel.

13:30 Fold the dough a second time.

14:00 Fold the dough a third time.

14:30 Fold the dough a fourth time.

16:30 Divide the dough in two. Preshape.

17:00 Final shape. Prepare a plate or tray with the porridge. After you've made the final shape, spray or brush the dough with water and then take the entire dough and roll it in the porridge. Then place the dough pieces in proofing baskets as usual with the seam face up. Place a plastic bag over the baskets and place in the refrigerator.

Bake the next day. Preheat your baking sheet and the pot with the lid on for 1 hour in an oven set to 480°F (250°C), using the top and bottom elements. Score the bread, place it in the pot, and put the lid on. Reduce the heat to 450°F (230°C). After 20 minutes, remove the lid and bake for another 20 minutes. Repeat the procedure for the second bread.

Rye porridge bread with raisins

This has long been one of my favorite breads, in all categories. You can absolutely leave out the raisins if you want. But believe me, rye + raisins = love.

Weight		Ingredients	Baker's percentage
total flour weight: 28 ¼ oz.	(800 g)	for 2 breads	100 %
2 ¾ oz.	(80 g)	wholemeal rye flour	10 %
12 ⅔ oz.	(360 g)	bread flour	45 %
12 ⅔ oz.	(360 g)	sifted heritage wheat flour	45 %
20 ½ oz.	(580 g)	water	72.5 %
5 ½ oz.	(160 g)	sourdough	20 %
¾ oz.	(20 g)	salt	2.5 %
4 ¼ oz.	(120 g)	groats	15 %
8 ½ oz.	(240 g)	water (for groats)	30 %
4 ¼ oz.	(120 g)	raisins	15 %
		+ extra groats to cover the bread with	

The night before you're going to make the dough, boil 8 ½ ounces (240 g) of water and blanch 4 ¼ ounces (120 g) of groats. Put the lid on. Let it stand until the next day.

11:00 Place the raisins in a small bowl and pour just enough water (from the total amount of water in the recipe) to cover them.

12:00 Mix together the water, sourdough, and flour in a bowl. Cover with a lid / kitchen towel.

12:30 Mix the raisins and water (in which they were soaked) together with the salt and porridge into the dough. Cover with a lid / kitchen towel.

13:00 Fold the dough over itself. Take one edge of the dough, pull it up, and fold it over itself. Rotate the bowl a quarter turn and repeat until you've folded all the dough. Cover with a lid / kitchen towel.

13:30 Fold the dough a second time.

14:00 Fold the dough a third time.

14:30 Fold the dough a fourth time.

16:30 Divide the dough in two. Preshape.

17:00 Final shape. Prepare a plate or tray with the porridge. After you've made the final shape, spray or brush the dough with water and then take the entire dough and roll it in the porridge. Then place the dough in proofing baskets with the seam face up. Place a plastic bag over the baskets and place in the refrigerator.

Bake the next day. Preheat your baking sheet and the pot with the lid on for 1 hour in an oven set to 480°F (250°C), using the top and bottom elements. Score the bread, place it in the pot, and put the lid on. Reduce the heat to 450°F (230°C). After 20 minutes, remove the lid and bake for another 20 minutes. Repeat the procedure for the second bread.

Spelt porridge bread

I usually hold back a little of the water when baking with spelt as the flour is often a little softer. However, my stone-ground, sifted spelt flour absorbs a relatively large amount of water, so it works well. If you use milled, sifted spelt flour, it may be a good idea to hold back a little water when first mixing.

Weight		Ingredients	Baker's percentage
total flour weight: 28 ¼ oz.	(800 g)	for 2 breads	100 %
2 ¾ oz.	(80 g)	wholemeal spelt flour	10 %
14 oz.	(400 g)	stone-ground sifted spelt flour	50 %
11 ¼ oz.	(320 g)	sifted heritage wheat flour	40 %
19 ¾ oz.	(560 g)	water	70 %
5 ½ oz.	(160 g)	sourdough	20 %
¾ oz.	(20 g)	salt	2.5 %
4 ¼ oz.	(120 g)	spelt groats	15 %
8 ½ oz.	(240 g)	water (for groats)	30 %
		+ extra groats to cover the bread with	

The night before you're going to make the dough, boil 8 ½ ounces (240 g) of water and blanch 4 ¼ ounces (120 g) of groats. Put the lid on and let it stand until the next day.

12:00 Mix almost all the water, sourdough, and flour together in a bowl. Cover with a lid / kitchen towel.

12:30 Mix in the salt, porridge, and remaining water. Cover with a lid / kitchen towel.

13:00 Fold the dough over itself. Take one edge of the dough, pull it up, and fold it over itself. Rotate the bowl a quarter turn and repeat until you've folded all the dough. Cover with a lid / kitchen towel.

13:30 Fold the dough a second time.

14:00 Fold the dough a third time.

14:30 Fold the dough a fourth time.

16:30 Divide the dough in two. Preshape.

17:00 Final shape. Prepare a plate or tray with the porridge. After you've made the final shape, spray or brush the dough with water and then take the entire dough and roll it in the porridge. Then place the dough pieces in proofing baskets as usual with the seam face up. Place a plastic bag over the baskets and place in the refrigerator.

Bake the next day. Preheat your baking sheet and the pot with the lid on for 1 hour in an oven set to 480°F (250°C), using the top and bottom elements. Score the bread, place it in the pot, and put the lid on. Reduce the heat to 450°F (230°C). After 20 minutes, remove the lid and bake for another 20 minutes. Repeat the procedure for the second bread.

Einkorn porridge bread

When you toast groats, you lose some of the creaminess they otherwise add to the final bread. By toasting half of the groats you get the best of three worlds. Creaminess, flavor, and texture.

Weight	Ingredients	Baker's percentage
total flour weight: 28 ¼ oz. (800 g)	for 2 breads	100 %
5 ⅔ oz. (160 g)	wholemeal einkorn flour	20 %
11 ¼ oz. (320 g)	bread flour	40 %
11 ¼ oz. (320 g)	sifted heritage wheat flour	40 %
19 ¾ oz. (560 g)	water	70 %
5 ½ oz. (160 g)	sourdough	20 %
¾ oz. (20 g)	salt	2.5 %
4 ¼ oz. (120 g)	einkorn groats	15 %
8 ½ oz. (240 g)	water (for groats)	30 %
	+ extra groats to cover the bread with	

The night before you're going to make the dough, weigh out the groats and water for blanching. Toast half of the groats on a sheet pan in a fan-assisted oven at 350°F (175°C) for 10–15 minutes. Then mix the toasted groats with the untoasted ones and pour boiling water over them. Stir a little and then put a lid on.

12:00 Mix almost all the water, sourdough, and flour together in a bowl. Cover with a lid / kitchen towel.

12:30 Mix in the salt, porridge, and remaining water. Cover with a lid / kitchen towel.

13:00 Fold the dough over itself. Take one edge of the dough, pull it up, and fold it over itself. Rotate the bowl a quarter turn and repeat until you've folded all the dough. Cover with a lid / kitchen towel.

13:30 Fold the dough a second time.

14:00 Fold the dough a third time.

14:30 Fold the dough a fourth time.

16:30 Divide the dough in two. Preshape.

17:00 Final shape. Prepare a plate or tray with the porridge. After you've made the final shape, spray or brush the dough with water and then take the entire dough and roll it in the porridge. Then place the dough pieces in proofing baskets as usual with the seam face up. Place a plastic bag over the baskets and place in the refrigerator.

Bake the next day. Preheat your baking sheet and the pot with the lid on for 1 hour in an oven set to 480°F (250°C), using the top and bottom elements. Score the bread, place it in the pot, and put the lid on. Reduce the heat to 450°F (230°C). After 20 minutes, remove the lid and bake for another 20 minutes. Repeat the procedure for the second bread.

Porridge bread with cranberries & raisins

This bread is a creamy, slightly chewy porridge bread. I love the sweetness of the raisins combined with the tartness of the cranberries and the lightly toasted flavor of the bread.

Weight		Ingredients	Baker's percentage
total flour weight: 28 ¼ oz.	(800 g)	for 2 breads	100 %
3 ½ oz.	(100 g)	wholemeal emmer flour	12.5 %
12 ⅓ oz.	(350 g)	bread flour	43.75 %
12 ⅓ oz.	(350 g)	sifted heritage wheat flour	43.75 %
20 ½ oz.	(580 g)	water	72.5 %
5 ½ oz.	(160 g)	sourdough	20 %
¾ oz.	(20 g)	salt	2.5 %
4 ¼ oz.	(120 g)	four-grain groats	15 %
8 ½ oz.	(240 g)	water (for groats)	30 %
2 oz.	(60 g)	dried cranberries	7.5 %
2 oz.	(60 g)	raisins	7.5 %
		+ oatmeal to cover the bread with	

Boil the four-grain groats the night before, you're going to make the dough. Bring 8 ½ ounces (240 g) of water to a boil, pour in 4 ¼ ounces (120 g) of crushed four-grain groats, and stir constantly as it quickly turns into a porridge-like consistency that easily burns in the saucepan. Once all the water has been absorbed, after about 5 minutes, remove the saucepan from the stove, put on a lid, and leave until the next day.

11:00 Place the raisins in a bowl and pour just enough water (from the total amount of water in the recipe) to cover them. Place the cranberries in another bowl (they don't need to be soaked).

12:00 Mix together the water, sourdough, and flour in a bowl. Cover with a lid / kitchen towel.

12:30 Mix the cranberries and the soaked raisins (including the water) together with the salt and porridge into the dough. Cover with a lid / kitchen towel.

13:00 Fold the dough over itself. Take one edge of the dough, pull it up, and fold it over itself. Rotate the bowl a quarter turn and repeat until you've folded all the dough. Cover with a lid / kitchen towel.

13:30 Fold the dough a second time.

14:00 Fold the dough a third time.

14:30 Fold the dough a fourth time.

16:30 Divide the dough in two. Preshape.

17:00 Final shape. Prepare a plate of oatmeal. After you've made the final shape, spray the dough pieces with water and then take them and roll in the oatmeal. Then place the dough pieces in proofing baskets as usual with the seam face up. Place a plastic bag over it and place in the refrigerator.

Bake the next day. Preheat your baking sheet and the pot with the lid on for 1 hour in an oven set to 480°F (250°C), using the top and bottom elements. Score the bread, place it in the pot, and put the lid on. Reduce the heat to 450°F (230°C). After 20 minutes, remove the lid and bake for another 20 minutes. Repeat the procedure for the second bread.

Whole grain

A delicious medium-coarse bread with extra chewiness from the whole grains. For this, I use whole spelt grains, which I cook the night before. This increases the digestibility and the soaking process makes the bread juicy in flavor.

Weight		Ingredients	Baker's percentage
total flour weight: 28 ¼ oz.	(800 g)	for 2 breads	100 %
8 ½ oz.	(240 g)	wholemeal emmer flour	30 %
7 oz.	(200 g)	stone-ground sifted spelt flour	25 %
12 ⅔ oz.	(360 g)	bread flour	45 %
19 ¾ oz.	(560 g)	water	70 %
5 ½ oz.	(160 g)	sourdough	20 %
¾ oz.	(20 g)	salt	2.5 %
5 ⅔ oz.	(160 g)	wholemeal spelt	20 %
+ 11 ⅓ oz.	(320 g)	water for boiling	

Boil the whole grains the night before you're going to make the dough. Bring to a boil and simmer for about 15 minutes to ensure there are no hard pieces left. Cover with a lid and leave until the next day.

12:00 Mix almost all the water, sourdough, and flour together in a bowl. Cover with a lid/kitchen towel.

12:30 Mix in the salt, the whole grains, and the remaining water. Cover with a lid/kitchen towel.

13:00 Fold the dough over itself. Take one edge of the dough, pull it up, and fold it over itself. Rotate the bowl a quarter turn and repeat until you've folded all the dough. Cover with a lid/kitchen towel.

13:30 Fold the dough a second time.

14:00 Fold the dough a third time.

14:30 Fold the dough a fourth time.

16:30 Divide the dough in two. Preshape.

17:00 Final shape. Place a plastic bag over the baskets and place in the refrigerator.

Bake the next day. Preheat your baking sheet and the pot with the lid on for 1 hour in an oven set to 480°F (250°C), using the top and bottom elements. Score the bread, place it in the pot, and put the lid on. Reduce the heat to 450°F (230°C). After 20 minutes, remove the lid and bake for another 20 minutes. Repeat the procedure for the second bread.

Danish rye bread

My version of a classic Danish unsweetened rye bread. Perfect for sandwiches.

Weight		Ingredients	Baker's percentage
total flour weight: 28 ¼ oz.	(800 g)	for 2 breads in 35 fl. oz. (1.5 l) molds	100 %
22 ½ oz.	(640 g)	wholemeal rye flour	80 %
5 ⅔ oz.	(160 g)	sifted heritage wheat flour	20 %
26 ⅔ oz.	(760 g)	water	95 %
11 ¼ oz.	(320 g)	sourdough	40 %
¾ oz.	(20 g)	salt	2.5 %
8 ½ oz.	(240 g)	whole rye grains	30 %
+ 17 oz.	(480 g)	water for boiling	
4 ¼ oz.	(120 g)	sunflower hearts	15 %
1 ⅓ oz.	(40 g)	flax seeds	5 %

Boil the rye grains the night before you're going to make the dough. Bring to a boil and simmer for about 15 minutes. Cover with a lid and leave until the next day.

Weigh the flax seeds and sunflower hearts in the bowl you plan to use for baking the next day. Pour in almost all the water (hold back about 1 ¾ ounces / 50 g). Put a lid on and leave to stand until the next day.

12:00 In the bowl with the seed mixture and water, mix in the sourdough, rye grains, and flour. Mix in a machine for a few minutes until everything is well mixed, or mix thoroughly by hand until everything is well combined. Cover with a lid / kitchen towel.

12:30 Mix in the salt and the remaining water. Cover with a lid / kitchen towel.

14:00 With wet hands, divide the dough in two and place each half in a pan lined with baking paper. Wet your hands further and flatten and iron out the top so it's nice and smooth.

16:30 Make sure the dough has risen by about half an inch (1–2 cm) and is bulging upward. Place in the refrigerator until the next day.

Bake the next day. Preheat the oven for 1 hour at 430°F (220°C), using the top and bottom elements, before putting the bread in. Also, put a rack in the middle of the oven.

When it's time to bake, take a potato skewer or similar and prick the bread all the way to the bottom. As a reference, that's about ten sticks evenly spaced out. Place the molds in the oven and lower the heat to 410°F (210°C). Bake for 75 minutes. If you have a probe thermometer, the internal temperature of the bread should be 210°F (100°C). Remove the bread from the molds, wrap each in a kitchen towel, and let cool. These breads need a longer time to rest before slicing. I think 10–12 hours is about right. They can be quite chewy but also crumble if you slice them too soon.

Kavring

This is my recipe for a typical Swedish dark rye bread, Kavring. This dough is very sticky with all the ingredients, so it's easiest to mix the whole dough together right away.

Weight		Ingredients	Baker's percentage
total flour weight: 28 ¼ oz.	(800 g)	for 2 breads in 35 fl. oz. (1.5 l) molds	100 %
11 ¼ oz.	(320 g)	wholemeal rye flour	40 %
11 ¼ oz.	(320 g)	sifted heritage wheat flour	40 %
5 ⅔ oz.	(160 g)	unblended sifted rye flour	20 %
17 oz.	(480 g)	water	60 %
11 ¼ oz.	(320 g)	sourdough	40 %
⅔ oz.	(18 g)	salt	2.25 %
8 ½ oz.	(240 g)	rye groats	30 %
+ 17 oz.	(480 g)	water for boiling	
5 ⅔ oz.	(160 g)	dark syrup	20 %
1 ⅓ oz.	(40 g)	roasted malt syrup / liquid wort	5 %
4 g		whole ground cumin	0,5 %

The night before you're going to make the dough, boil 8 ½ ounces (240 g) of rye groats in 4 ¼ ounces (480 g) of water. Bring the water to a boil, pour in the rye groats, and stir constantly as it quickly turns into a porridge-like consistency that easily burns in the saucepan. Once all the water has been absorbed, after about 5 minutes, remove the saucepan from the stove, put on a lid, and leave until the next day.

12:00 Mix all the ingredients together. Mix in a machine for a few minutes until everything is well mixed, or mix thoroughly by hand until everything is well combined. Cover with a lid / kitchen towel.

14:00 With wet hands, divide the dough in two and place each half in a pan lined with baking paper. Wet your hands further and flatten and iron out the top so it's nice and somewhat smooth.

17:00 Once the dough has risen by about ½ inch (1–2 cm) and is bulging upward, place it in the refrigerator.

Bake the next day. Preheat the oven for 1 hour at 430°F (220°C), using the top and bottom elements, before putting the bread in. Also, put a rack in the middle of the oven.

When it's time to bake, take a potato skewer or similar and prick the bread all the way to the bottom. As a reference, that's about ten sticks evenly spaced out. Place the molds in the oven and lower the heat to 410°F (210°C). Bake for about 75 minutes. If you have a probe thermometer, the internal temperature of the bread should be 210°F (100°C). Turn the bread out from the molds, wrap each in a kitchen towel, and leave to cool. These breads need to rest for at least half a day before slicing.

Seeds

This aromatic bread is a real powerhouse. The grains provide valuable fiber, vitamins, and minerals. A delight that not only tastes good but is also good for you.

Weight		Ingredients	Baker's percentage
total flour weight: 28 ¼ oz.	(800 g)	for 2 breads in 35 fl. oz. (1.5 l) molds	100 %
19 ¾ oz.	(560 g)	wholemeal einkorn flour	70 %
8 ½ oz.	(240 g)	wholemeal spelt flour	30 %
26 ⅔ oz.	(760 g)	water	95 %
8 ½ oz.	(240 g)	sourdough	30 %
¾ oz.	(20 g)	salt	2.5 %
5 ⅔ oz.	(160 g)	whole spelt grains	20 %
2 ¾ oz.	(80 g)	sunflower hearts	10 %
+ 11 ⅓ oz.	(320 g)	water (for boiling)	
2 ¾ oz.	(80 g)	pumpkin seeds	10 %
1 ⅓ oz.	(40 g)	flax seeds	5 %
1 ⅓ oz.	(40 g)	sesame seeds	5 %
1 ⅓ oz.	(40 g)	water	5 %
		+ additional seeds and kernels to cover the bread with	

The night before you're going to make the dough, boil 5 ½ ounces (160 g) of spelt grains in 11 ¼ ounces (320 g) of water. Simmer for about 15 minutes to ensure there are no hard pieces left. Cover with a lid and leave until the next day.

Weigh the seeds, pumpkin seeds, and sunflower hearts in a bowl. Add almost all the water (hold back about 1 ¾ ounces/50 g) and put on a lid. Leave this until the next day as well.

12:00 Mix the sourdough, flour, and whole spelt grains into the seed and water mixture. Mix in a machine for a few minutes until everything is well mixed, or mix thoroughly by hand until everything is combined. Cover with a lid/kitchen towel.

12:30 Mix in the salt and the remaining water. Cover with a lid/kitchen towel.

14:00 With moistened hands, divide the dough into two parts. Place each into their own mold lined with a sheet of baking paper. Wet your hands further and flatten and iron out the top so it's nice and somewhat smooth. Spray some water on top and sprinkle the seeds on top of that.

16:30 Once the dough has risen by about ½ inch (1–2 cm) and is bulging upward, place the molds in the refrigerator.

Bake the next day. Preheat the oven for 1 hour at 430°F (220°C), using the top and bottom elements, before putting the bread in. Also, put a rack in the middle of the oven.

When it's time to bake, take a potato skewer and prick the bread all the way to the bottom. About ten sticks evenly spaced out is enough. Place the molds in the oven and lower the heat to 410°F (210°C). Bake for about 75 minutes. If you have a probe thermometer, the internal temperature of the bread should be 210°F (100°C). Turn the breads out from the molds, wrap them in kitchen towels, and leave to cool. The breads need to rest for a few hours before slicing.

Rye-wheat bread

A medium-coarse and delicious flatbread with equal parts rye and wheat. It's a versatile base for any meal, from breakfast to dinner.

Weight		Ingredients	Baker's percentage
total flour weight: 28 ¼ oz.	(800 g)	for 2 breads in 35 fl. oz. (1.5 l) molds	100 %
14 oz.	(400 g)	wholemeal landrace rye flour	50 %
14 oz.	(400 g)	sifted heritage wheat flour	50 %
21 ¾ oz.	(620 g)	water	77.5 %
11 ¼ oz.	(320 g)	sourdough	40 %
⅔ oz.	(18 g)	salt	2.25 %
8 ½ oz.	(240 g)	rye groats	30 %
+ 17 oz.	(480 g)	water for boiling	
		+ rye bran to top the bread with	

Boil the rye groats the night before you're going to make the dough. Bring 17 ounces (480 g) of water to a boil, pour in the rye groats, and stir constantly, as it quickly turns into a porridge-like consistency that easily burns in the saucepan. Once all the water has been absorbed, after about 5 minutes, remove the saucepan from the stove, put on a lid, and leave until the next day.

12:00 Mix together almost all the water (hold back about 1 ¾ ounces / 50 g), the boiled rye groats, the sourdough, and the flour in a bowl. Cover with a lid / kitchen towel.

12:30 Mix in the salt and the remaining water. Cover with a lid / kitchen towel.

14:00 With wet hands, divide the dough in two and place each half in a pan lined with baking paper. Wet your hands further and flatten and iron out the top so it's somewhat even. Sprinkle rye bran on top of the bread.

16:30 Once the dough has risen by about ½ inch (1–2 cm) and is bulging upward, place the molds in the refrigerator.

Bake the next day. Preheat the oven for 1 hour at 430°F (220°C), using the top and bottom elements, before putting the bread in. Also, put a rack in the middle of the oven.

When it's time to bake, take a potato skewer or similar and prick the bread all the way to the bottom. As a reference, that's about 10 sticks evenly spaced out. Place the molds in the oven and reduce the temperature to 410°F (210°C). Bake for 75 minutes. If you have a probe thermometer, the internal temperature of the bread should be 210°F (100°C). Turn the bread out from the molds, wrap each in a kitchen towel, and leave to cool. These breads ideally need to rest for half a day before slicing.

Sweet pastry

When I bake buns and other sweet pastry, I use regular yeast. There are several reasons, but mainly it's because it makes for a better (and tastier) end result. With yeast, the buns turn out just as soft, airy, and delicious as I want them to be. As you know, sourdough has an acidic taste and I want to avoid that in sweet pastry.

The most important thing when baking buns is to let them proof enough. As a rule, the buns should double in size before going into the oven. This makes them as fluffy and light as possible. If the buns don't look particularly large when you plan to bake them, wait another hour or as long as needed.

Cinnamon buns

The beloved cinnamon bun ... the bun of buns.

Weight		Ingredients	Baker's percentage
total flour weight: 28 ¼ oz.	(800 g)	for 16–20 buns	100 %
28 ¼ oz.	(800 g)	bread flour	100 %
4 ¼ oz.	(120 g)	butter, room temperature	15 %
½ oz.	(12 g)	whole cardamom seeds	1.5 %
14 oz.	(400 g)	milk, 3 % fat content	50 %
		1 egg	
½ oz.	(16 g)	fresh yeast	2 %
4 ¼ oz.	(120 g)	sugar	15 %
⅓ oz.	(10 g)	salt	1.25 %
		+ pearl sugar	

Cinnamon filling:

5 ⅔ oz.	(160 g)	butter, room temperature
4 oz.	(112 g)	raw cane sugar
½ oz.	(16 g)	Ceylon cinnamon
½ oz.	(16 g)	wheat flour

Syrup:

2 ⅔ oz.	(75 g)	raw cane sugar
3 ½ oz.	(100 g)	water

Pour all the ingredients for the **filling** into a bowl and mix together with a fork.

Bring the sugar and water to a boil for the **syrup.** Allow to cool.

Take out the butter a good few hours before you knead the **dough,** as it's easier if it's at room temperature. I always take out my butter the night before.

The buns will taste much better if you use whole cardamom seeds that you crush or mortar yourself. Leave the milk and eggs cold so that proofing doesn't start too quickly.

Dissolve the yeast in the milk. Then mix the remaining ingredients in a food processor / mixer and knead the dough for about 5 minutes, until smooth and well-combined. There should be no visible lumps of butter or flour. The dough will be sticky at this point, but that's fine.

Flour the counter and roll out the dough. Shape into an even ball.

Flatten the dough so that it cools faster in the refrigerator. Flour, wrap in plastic, and place in a mold. Let the dough rest in the refrigerator for 1 hour.

Take out the dough, flour the counter, and roll the dough out into a large rectangle about ½ inch (1 cm) thick.

Spread the filling evenly over all the dough. Triple-fold it as in the pictures on the right.

Roll out the entire package further. The dough should be about ½ inch (1–2 cm) thick.

Cut out strips with a pizza slicer or a large dough scraper. My strips/buns usually weigh about 3 ounces (85 g) each.

Take a strip and pull it out a little, as far as the dough will allow. Don't overdo it so that the dough cracks. Twist the strip around itself and shape into buns (see the pictures on page 132). Evenly space out the buns on two sheet pans lined with baking paper.

Cover the sheets with plastic wrap and place them low down in the refrigerator until the next day. If your sheet pans don't fit in the refrigerator, you can place the buns closer together in a suitable mold covered with plastic wrap. The next day (when the buns are cold and hard) it's easier to take them out one by one and space them out evenly on sheet pans. (If you want to bake the buns the same day, you don't need to wrap them in plastic or place them in the refrigerator. Just let them proof at room temperature until double in size.)

Remove the plastic wrap and place the trays in the oven with the light on but no heat, and place a small bowl of hot water at the bottom.

Let the buns proof for 2–4 hours. They should get really big, about double in size.

Take the buns out and preheat your oven for 1 hour at 480°F (225°C), using the top and bottom elements.

Spray the buns with a little water and sprinkle with pearl sugar.

Bake one sheet at a time in the center of the oven for 8–12 minutes, until the buns turn golden brown. Brush with sugar syrup immediately after the buns come out of the oven.

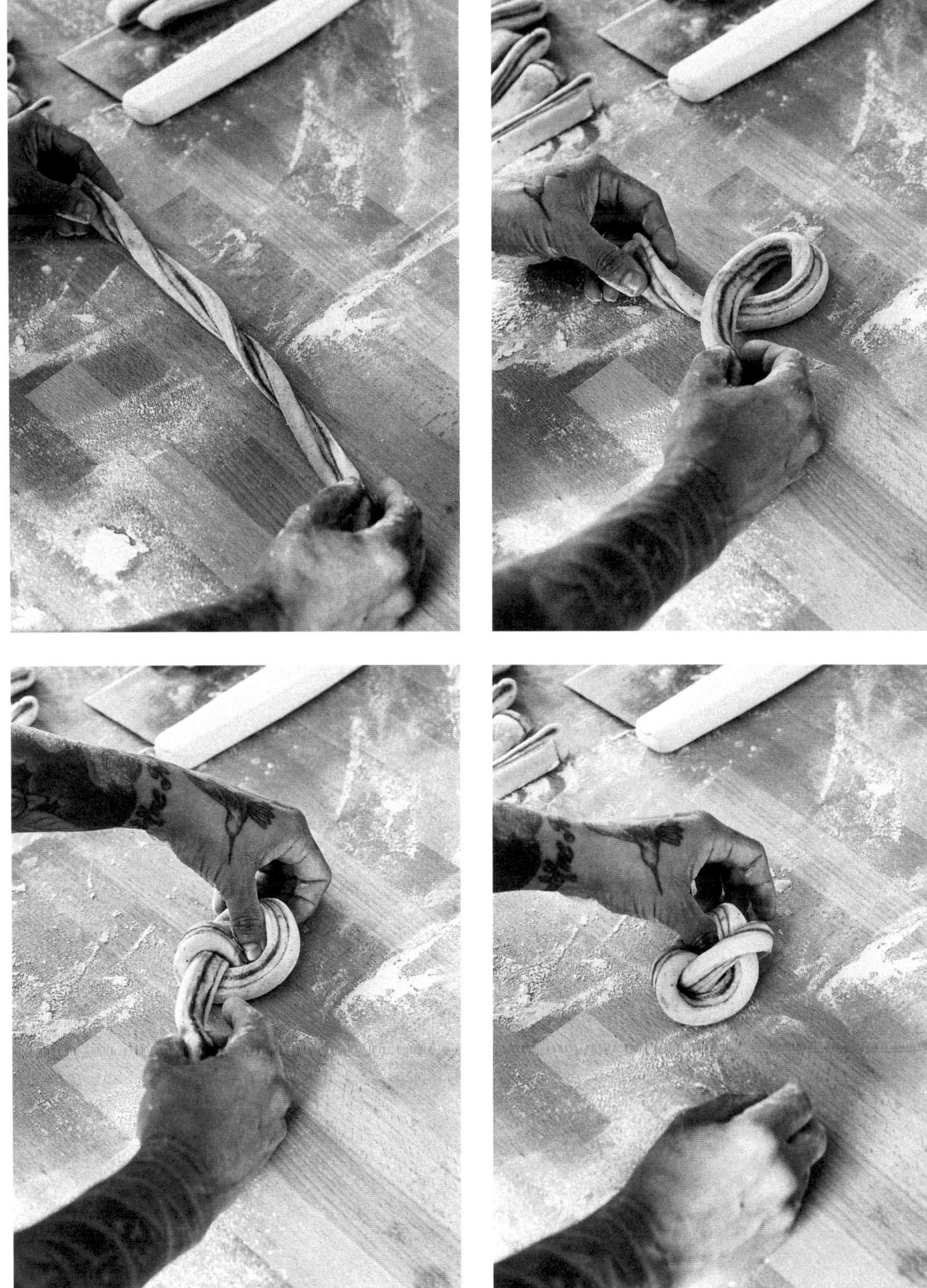

Cardamom buns

A modern classic. This is the same bun dough as for the cinnamon buns. What changes is the filling and what we put on the buns before they go into the oven.

Weight		Ingredients	Baker's percentage
total flour weight: 28 ¼ oz.	(800 g)	for 16–20 buns	100 %
28 ¼ oz.	(800 g)	bread flour	100 %
4 ¼ oz.	(120 g)	butter, room temperature	15 %
½ oz.	(12 g)	whole cardamom seeds	1.5 %
14 oz.	(400 g)	milk, 3 % fat content	50 %
		1 egg	
½ oz.	(16 g)	fresh yeast	2 %
4 ¼ oz.	(120 g)	sugar	15 %
⅓ oz.	(10 g)	salt	1.25 %
		+ mortared cardamom	
		+ icing sugar before baking	

Cardamom filling:

5 ⅔ oz.	(160 g)	butter, room temperature
4 oz.	(112 g)	raw cane sugar
¼ oz.	(8 g)	ground cardamom
1 oz.	(25 g)	wheat flour

Syrup:

2 ⅔ oz.	(75 g)	raw cane sugar
3 ½ oz.	(100 g)	water

Pour all the ingredients for the **filling** into a bowl and mix together with a fork.

Bring the sugar and water to a boil for the **syrup.** Allow to cool.

Mix together a handful of sugar and some ground cardamom in a bowl. A little vanilla sugar is also good.

Take out the butter a good few hours before you knead the **dough,** as it's easier if it's at room temperature. I always take out my butter the night before.

The buns will taste much better if you use whole cardamom seeds that you crush or mortar yourself. Leave the milk and eggs cold so that proofing doesn't start too quickly.

Dissolve the yeast in the milk. Then mix the remaining ingredients in a food processor / mixer and knead the dough for about 5 minutes, until smooth and well-combined. There should be no visible lumps of butter or flour. The dough will be sticky at this point, but that's fine.

Flour the counter and roll out all the dough. Shape into an even ball.

Flatten the dough so that it cools faster in the refrigerator. Flour, wrap in plastic, and place in a mold. Leave to rest in the refrigerator for 1 hour.

Take out the dough, flour the counter, and roll the dough out into a large rectangle about ½ inch (1 cm) thick.

Spread the filling evenly over all the dough. Triple-fold it as in the pictures on page 131.

Roll out the dough further. The dough should be about ½ inch (1–2 cm) thick.

Cut out strips with a pizza slicer or a large dough scraper. My strips/buns usually weigh about 3 ounces (85 g) each.

Take a strip and pull it out a little, as far as the dough will allow. Don't overdo it so that the dough cracks. Twist the strip around itself and shape into buns (see the pictures on page 132). Evenly space out the buns on two sheet pans lined with baking paper.

Cover the sheets with plastic wrap and place them low down in the refrigerator until the next day. If your sheet pans don't fit in the refrigerator, you can place the buns closer together in a suitable mold covered with plastic wrap. The next day (when the buns are cold and hard) it's easier to take them out one by one and space them out evenly on sheet pans. (If you want to bake the buns the same day, you don't need to wrap them in plastic or place them in the refrigerator. Just let them proof at room temperature until double in size.)

Remove the plastic wrap and place the trays in the oven with the light on, but with no heat. Place a small bowl of hot water inside.

Let the buns proof for 2–4 hours. They should get really big, about double in size.

Take the buns out and preheat your oven for 1 hour at 480°F (225°C), using the top and bottom elements.

Spray the buns with a little water and sprinkle with the cardamom sugar mixture.

Bake one sheet at a time in the center of the oven for 8–12 minutes, until the buns turn golden brown. Brush with sugar syrup immediately after the buns come out of the oven.

Tip: It's a good idea to have a vanilla pod to hand that you can split and scrape out and let boil with the syrup. If so, make a larger batch of syrup in about 18 ounces (500 g) of water. The sugar syrup will last a long time in the refrigerator if stored in an airtight jar.

Vanilla buns

You can turn the cardamom bun into a vanilla bun by adding some homemade vanilla cream before they go into the oven. It's as tasty as it sounds. Perhaps even tastier ...

Vanilla cream:

4 ¼ oz.	(120 g)	egg yolks
1 ¼ oz.	(35 g)	cornstarch
4 ½ oz.	(125 g)	sugar
		1 vanilla pod
17 ⅔ oz.	(500 g)	milk, 3 % fat content
1 ¾ oz.	(50 g)	butter

Follow the recipe for cardamom buns, but before you put the buns in the oven, press a generous dollop of vanilla cream into the center of the buns using a piping bag.

Quickly whisk together the egg yolks, cornstarch, and half of the sugar in a bowl. Half a minute with an electric whisk is usually enough.

Split the vanilla pod lengthwise and scrape out the contents. Add the milk, pour in the rest of the sugar, and bring to the boil in a saucepan. Set aside and let the milk mixture cool for 5–10 minutes.

Pour the milk mixture into the egg mixture and whisk until everything is combined.

Then pour everything back into the saucepan and bring to a boil, stirring constantly.

Remove the saucepan from the heat once the cream thickens. Add the butter and continue stirring until all the butter has melted into the cream. Pour into a clean bowl, cover with plastic wrap, and place in the refrigerator.

Unfortunately, vanilla cream doesn't last very long even if kept in the refrigerator. It breaks down and often goes bad after just 2–3 days. Therefore, I usually make vanilla cream no more than a day before I plan to use it.

Semmel buns

A handcrafted semmel bun inspired by the master, Sébastien Boudet. Ultimately, it's the almond paste that makes all the difference. Of course, it doesn't hurt to have a delicious bun and delicious whipped cream as well! If you've never tried making your own almond paste, I highly recommend you try it. It really is something else!

Weight		Ingredients	Baker's percentage
total flour weight: 28 ¼ oz.	(800 g)	for about 20 semmel buns	100 %
28 ¼ oz.	(800 g)	bread flour	100 %
8 ½ oz.	(240 g)	butter, room temperature	30 %
½ oz.	(12 g)	cardamom	1.5 %
14 oz.	(400 g)	milk, 3 % fat content	50 %
		1 egg	
½ oz.	(16 g)	fresh yeast	2 %
5 ⅔ oz.	(160 g)	sugar	20 %
⅓ oz.	(10 g)	salt	1.25 %

Almond paste:

8 ¾ oz.	(250 g)	sweet almonds
7 oz.	(200 g)	raw cane sugar
		a pinch (1–2 g) salt
		+ zest and juice from ½ orange
		+ zest and juice from 1 lemon
3 ½ oz.	(100 g)	water
		+ a few dashes of heavy cream (stir in just before using the almond paste

To garnish:

3 cups	(750 ml)	heavy cream
		+ icing sugar when assembling

Toast half of the almonds for the **almond paste** on a sheet pan in the oven at 400°F (200°C) for about 15 minutes. They should take on a nice color and flavor, and smoke a little.

Mix the almonds, sugar, and salt, and the zest and juice from the orange and lemon. Dilute with water until you get the right consistency. The almond paste should be relatively runny. This is partly because the almonds absorb liquid as the paste mellows in the refrigerator, and partly because the bun itself will absorb the liquid. Therefore, it tastes better if the almond paste is runny instead of dry once the bun is assembled.

When it's time to use the almond paste, pour in a few dashes of unwhipped heavy cream and stir until you get the right consistency. The cream also usually helps to round off the flavors nicely. Remember that the cream will shorten the shelf life of the almond paste, so only add it if you're planning to use the almond paste in the next few days.

Take out the butter for the bun dough a good few hours before you knead the dough, as it's easier if it's at room temperature. I always take out my butter the night before.

The buns will taste much better if you use whole cardamom seeds that you crush or mortar yourself. Leave the milk and eggs cold so that proofing doesn't start too quickly.

Dissolve the yeast in the milk. Then mix the remaining ingredients in a food processor / mixer and knead the dough for about 5 minutes, or for as long as it takes for the dough to become smooth and well-combined. There should be no visible lumps of butter or flour. The dough will be sticky at this point but that's okay, provided it's well mixed.

Flour the counter and roll out all the dough. Shape into an even ball.

Flatten the dough so that it cools faster in the refrigerator. Flour, wrap in plastic, and place in a mold. Let the dough rest in the refrigerator for 1 hour.

Take out the dough, flour the counter, and cut small pieces weighing 2⅔ ounces (75 g) each. Roll the balls evenly against the counter with the palm of your hand. Evenly space out the buns on sheet pans lined with baking paper.

Cover the sheets with plastic wrap and place them low down in the refrigerator until the next day. If the sheet pans don't fit in the refrigerator, you can place the buns closer together in a suitable mold covered with plastic wrap. The next day (when the buns are cold and hard) it's easier to take them out one by one and space them out evenly on sheet pans. (If you want to bake the buns the same day, you don't need to wrap them in plastic or place them in the refrigerator. Just let them proof at room temperature until double in size.)

Remove the plastic wrap and place the trays in the oven with the light on, but with no heat. Place a small bowl of hot water inside.

Let the buns proof for 2–4 hours. They should get really big, about double in size.

Take the buns out and preheat your oven for 1 hour at 480°F (225°C), using the top and bottom elements.

Bake one sheet at a time in the center of the oven for 8–10 minutes, until the buns turn golden brown. Take out and allow to cool.

Whip the cream just before assembling the semmel buns. Whip nice and gently, especially toward the end. When the cream forms small peaks, it's ready. It's better to stop a little too early than too late. Whipped cream that is too stiff is never a success. Pour into a piping bag.

If you've made almond paste in advance, take it out of the refrigerator, stir it around a bit, and make sure the consistency is right. If it's too hard, pour in a little unwhipped heavy cream.

Cut a triangle out of each bun and remove the lids. Pour in the almond paste, top with cream, put the lid back on, and dust with icing sugar.

Saffron twists with vanilla & orange

I bake and sell these in the bakery in December. It's a twist on the traditional Swedish lussekatter buns.

Weight		Ingredients	Baker's percentage
total flour weight: 28 ¼ oz.	(800 g)	for 16–20 buns	100 %
28 ¼ oz.	(800 g)	bread flour	100 %
4 ¼ oz.	(120 g)	butter, room temperature	15 %
14 oz.	(400 g)	milk, 3 % fat content	50 %
		1 egg	
½ oz.	(16 g)	fresh yeast	2 %
0.5 g		saffron (1 packet)	0.0625 %
4 ¼ oz.	(120 g)	sugar	15 %
⅓ oz.	(10 g)	salt	1.25 %

Orange and vanilla filling:

5 ⅔ oz.	(160 g)	butter, room temperature
4 oz.	(112 g)	raw cane sugar
½ oz.	(16 g)	vanilla sugar
½ oz.	(16 g)	wheat flour
		+ zest from 1 orange

Syrup:

2 ⅔ oz.	(75 g)	raw cane sugar
3 ½ oz.	(100 g)	water

Pour all the ingredients for the **filling** into a bowl and mix together with a fork.

Bring the sugar and water to a boil for the **syrup.** Allow to cool.

Take out the butter a few hours before you knead the **dough,** as it's easier if it's at room temperature. I always take out my butter the night before. Leave the milk and eggs cold so that proofing doesn't start too quickly.

Pour the milk into a mixer/food processor. Pour in the eggs, yeast, and saffron and mix for about 30 seconds until everything is combined. Then pour in the remaining ingredients and knead the dough for 5 minutes, until smooth and well-combined. There should be no visible lumps of butter or flour. The dough will be sticky at this point, but that's fine.

Flour the counter and roll out all the dough. Shape into an even ball.

Flatten the dough so that it cools faster in the refrigerator. Flour, wrap in plastic, and place in a mold. Let the dough rest in the refrigerator for 1 hour.

Take the dough out, flour the counter, and roll the dough out into a large rectangle. The dough should be about ½ inch (1 cm) thick.

Spread the filling evenly over all the dough. Triple-fold it as in the pictures on page 131.

Roll out the dough further. The dough should be about ½ inch (1–2 cm) thick.

Cut out strips with a pizza slicer or a large dough scraper. My strips/buns usually weigh about 3 ounces (85 g) each.

Take a strip and pull it out a little, as far as the dough will allow. Don't overdo it so that the dough cracks. Twist the strip around itself and shape into buns (see the pictures on page 132). Evenly space out the buns on sheet pans lined with baking paper.

Cover the sheets with plastic wrap and place them low down in the refrigerator until the next day. If the sheet pans don't fit in the refrigerator, you can place the buns closer together in a suitable mold covered with plastic wrap. The next day (when the buns are cold and hard) it's easier to take them out one by one and space them out evenly on sheet pans. (If you want to bake the buns the same day, you don't need to wrap them in plastic or place them in the refrigerator. Just let them proof at room temperature until double in size.)

Remove the plastic wrap and place the trays in the oven with the light on, but with no heat. Place a small bowl of hot water inside.

Let the buns proof for 2–4 hours. They should get really big, about double in size.

Take the buns out and preheat your oven for 1 hour at 480°F (225°C), using the top and bottom elements.

Spray the buns with a little water and sprinkle with some flaked almonds (if you like).

Bake one sheet at a time in the center of the oven for 8–12 minutes, until the buns turn golden brown. Brush with sugar syrup immediately after the buns come out of the oven.

Lussekatter buns

I rarely make traditional lussekatter buns at the bakery, but my family thinks it's fun to make them for Christmas, so here's my recipe. You can use the same basic recipe as for the saffron twists, but I like to use a little extra butter and sugar in the dough so that it's good enough on its own without any filling.

Weight		Ingredients	Baker's percentage
total flour weight: 28 ¼ oz.	(800 g)	for around 25 lussekatter buns	100 %
28 ¼ oz.	(800 g)	bread flour	100 %
8 ½ oz.	(240 g)	butter, room temperature	30 %
14 oz.	(400 g)	milk, 3 % fat content	50 %
		1 egg	
½ oz.	(16 g)	fresh yeast	2 %
0.5 g		saffron (1 packet)	0.0625 %
5 ⅔ oz.	(160 g)	sugar	20 %
¼ oz.	(8 g)	salt	1 %
		+ raisins	

Take out the butter a good few hours before you knead the dough, as it's easier if it's at room temperature. I always take out my butter the night before. Leave the milk and yeast cold so that proofing doesn't start too quickly.

Pour the milk into a mixer / food processor. Add the eggs, yeast, and saffron and mix for about 30 seconds until everything is combined. Then mix the remaining ingredients and knead the dough for 5–10 minutes, or for as long as it takes for the dough to become smooth and well-combined. There should be no visible lumps of butter or flour. The dough will be sticky at this point but that's okay, as long as it's well mixed.

Flour the counter and roll out all the dough. Shape into an even ball.

Flatten the dough so that it cools faster in the refrigerator. Flour, wrap in plastic, and place in a mold. Let the dough rest in the refrigerator for 1 hour.

Take out the dough, flour the counter, and cut small pieces weighing 2 ounces (60 g) each. Roll out small, even strips that are about ½ inch (1 cm) thick and then roll the sides in to give them the classic shape. Stick two raisins into each bun, if you like, to get that classic "cat's eyes" appearance. Evenly space out the buns on sheet pans lined with baking paper.

Cover the sheets with plastic wrap and place them low down in the refrigerator until the next day. If the sheet pans don't fit in the refrigerator, you can place the buns closer together in a suitable mold covered with plastic wrap. The next day (when the buns are cold and hard) it's easier to take them out one by one and space them out evenly on sheet pans. (If you want to bake the buns the same day, you don't need to wrap them in plastic or place them in the refrigerator. Just let them proof at room temperature until double in size.)

Remove the plastic wrap and place the trays in the oven with the light on, but with no heat. Place a small bowl of hot water inside.

Let the buns proof for 2–4 hours. They should get really big, about double in size.

Take the buns out and preheat your oven for 1 hour at 480°F (225°C), using the top and bottom elements.

Bake one sheet at a time in the center of the oven for 7–8 minutes, until they look baked. Cover the buns with a kitchen towel when they come out of the oven because they dry out quickly. I put the buns in plastic bags as soon as they've cooled.

Morning buns

Inspired by Chad Robertson. A type of croissant dough with butter filling and then rolled in sugar. Although it's not the easiest thing to hand roll croissant dough, once you taste it, you'll realize it was worth the effort. I've chosen to include two different fillings. Both are just as good in their own way.

Weight		Ingredients	Baker's percentage
total flour weight: 28 ¼ oz.	(800 g)	for around 16 buns	100 %
28 ¼ oz.	(800 g)	bread flour	100 %
1⅓ oz.	(40 g)	butter, room temperature	5 %
17 oz.	(480 g)	milk, 3 % fat content	60 %
		1 egg	
½ oz.	(16 g)	fresh yeast	2 %
2 ¾ oz.	(80 g)	raw cane sugar	10 %
½ oz.	(12 g)	salt	1.5 %
11¼ oz.	(320 g)	butter, room temperature (for rolling)	40 %

Cinnamon and orange filling:

5 ⅔ oz.	(160 g)	butter
4 oz.	(112 g)	raw cane sugar
½ oz.	(16 g)	Ceylon cinnamon
½ oz.	(16 g)	wheat flour
		+ zest from 1 orange

Poppy and lemon filling:

5 ⅔ oz.	(160 g)	butter
4 oz.	(112 g)	raw cane sugar
½ oz.	(16 g)	vanilla sugar
½ oz.	(16 g)	wheat flour
1¼ oz.	(32 g)	poppy seeds
		+ zest from 1 lemon

Choose one of them. Pour all the ingredients into a bowl and mix together with a fork.

Take out the butter a good few hours before you knead the **dough,** as it's easier if it's at room temperature. I always take out my butter the night before.

Leave the milk cold so that proofing doesn't start too quickly.

Dissolve the yeast in the milk. Then mix the remaining ingredients for the dough (apart from the butter for the rolling pin) in a food processor / mixer and knead the dough for about 5 minutes. While the dough is kneading, place the butter for the rolling pin between two sheets of baking paper. Roll out into a fairly even rectangle, about ½ inch (1 cm) thick. Then place the butter sheet in the refrigerator so that it hardens a little before you roll it into the dough.

Flour the counter and roll out all the dough. Shape into an even ball.

Flatten the dough a little, flour, cover with plastic wrap, and let it rest for about 10 minutes on the counter.

Roll out the dough into a larger rectangle than your butter sheet. The dough should be about ½ inch (1 cm) thick, just like the butter sheet.

Remove the baking paper from the butter and place it on the dough. Fold in the corners / edges of the dough and "seal" in the butter. Roll out into a large rectangle about ½ inch (1 cm) thick. Triple-fold it as in the pictures on page 131. Wrap the dough in plastic wrap and let it rest on the counter for 10 minutes.

Roll out the dough once more and triple-fold it. Wrap the dough in plastic wrap and place in the refrigerator. Rest for about 45 minutes.

Take the dough out, flour it, roll it out once more, and triple-fold it again. Wrap in plastic and place in the refrigerator. Rest for about 45 minutes.

Take the dough out again, flour it, and roll it out one last time. It should be a large oblong rectangle, about ½ inch (1 cm) thick.

Spread out the **filling** and roll the dough up like a Swiss roll. Start rolling from the long edge.

Cut out buns about 1 inch (2 cm) thick, about 3 ½–4 ounces (100–115 g) in weight.

Place the buns on a sheet of baking paper on a sheet pan with high edges. The buns should rise together when proofing and baking, so it's important to space them correctly depending on how big your buns are. I think it's a good idea to space them ½–1 inch (1.5–2 cm) apart in all directions. Then they usually rise nicely and create that characteristic square shape.

Cover the entire tray / mold with plastic wrap and place low down in the refrigerator until the next day. If the sheet pan doesn't fit in the refrigerator, you can place the buns closer together in a suitable mold instead. The next day (when the buns are cold and hard) it's easier to take them out one by one and space them out evenly on sheet pans. (If you want to bake the buns the same day, you don't need to wrap them in plastic or place them in the refrigerator. Just let them proof at room temperature.)

Remove the plastic wrap and place the trays in the oven with the light on, but with no heat. Place a small bowl of hot water inside.

Let the buns proof for 2–4 hours. They should be really big and have almost completely joined together when proofing.

Take the buns out and preheat your oven for 1 hour at 480°F (225°C), using the top and bottom elements.

Bake one sheet at a time in the center of the oven for about 15 minutes until the buns turn golden brown.

Take the buns out and let them cool slightly, so you can touch them without burning yourself. Then take them one by one and roll them in cinnamon sugar and place back on the sheet pan. (You can make cinnamon sugar by mixing some cinnamon and sugar in a bowl. I roll the poppy and lemon buns just in powdered sugar.)

Wiener buns

I make my Wiener buns from the same dough as the morning buns. I usually make them during the summer months and fill them with vanilla cream and garnish with fresh berries.

Weight		Ingredients	Baker's percentage
total flour weight: 28 ¼ oz.	(800 g)	for 12–16 Wiener buns	100 %
28 ¼ oz.	(800 g)	bread flour	100 %
1 ⅓ oz.	(40 g)	butter, room temperature	5 %
11 ¼ oz.	(320 g)	butter, room temperature (for rolling)	40 %
17 oz.	(480 g)	milk, 3 % fat content	60 %
½ oz.	(16 g)	fresh yeast	2 %
2 ¾ oz.	(80 g)	raw cane sugar	10 %
½ oz.	(12 g)	salt	1.5 %

Vanilla cream:

4 ¼ oz.	(120 g)	egg yolks
1 ¼ oz.	(35 g)	cornstarch
4 ½ oz.	(125 g)	sugar
		1 vanilla pod
17 ⅔ oz.	(500 g)	milk, 3 % fat content
1 ¾ oz.	(50 g)	butter

Glaze:

	icing sugar
	a few splashes of water

Quickly whisk together the egg yolks, cornstarch, and half of the sugar for the **vanilla cream** in a bowl. Half a minute with an electric whisk is usually enough.

Split the vanilla pod lengthwise and scrape out the contents. Add the milk, pour in the rest of the sugar, and bring to the boil in a saucepan. Set aside and let the milk mixture cool for 5–10 minutes.

Pour the milk mixture into the egg mixture and whisk until everything is combined.

Then pour everything back into the saucepan and bring to a boil, stirring constantly.

Remove the saucepan from the heat once the cream thickens. Add the butter and continue stirring until all the butter has melted into the cream. Pour into a clean bowl, cover with plastic wrap, and place in the refrigerator.

Unfortunately, vanilla cream doesn't last very long even if kept in the refrigerator. It breaks down and often goes bad after just 2–3 days. Therefore, I usually make vanilla cream no more than a day before I plan to use it.

Weigh out 3 ½–7 ounces (100–200 g) of icing sugar for the **glaze** in a bowl, then drizzle with water and stir with a spoon. Only add a few drops of water at a time because you only need very little. If you add too much water and the icing becomes too runny, add more icing sugar and vice versa.

Once you have a thick consistency, pour the glaze into a piping bag. If you don't have a piping bag, you can simply drizzle the glaze over the Wiener buns with a spoon.

Take out the butter for the **Wiener buns** a good few hours before you knead the dough, as it's easier if it's at room temperature. I always take out my butter the night before. Leave the milk cold so that proofing doesn't start too quickly.

Place the butter for the rolling pin between two sheets of baking paper and roll out into a fairly even rectangle, about ½ inch (1 cm) thick.

Dissolve the yeast in the milk. Then mix the remaining ingredients in a food processor / mixer and knead the dough for about 5 minutes. The dough will be sticky at this point but that's okay, provided it's well mixed.

Flour the counter and roll out all the dough. Shape into an even ball.

Flatten the dough a little, flour, cover with plastic wrap, and let it rest for about 10 minutes on the counter.

Roll out the dough into a larger rectangle than your butter sheet. The dough should be about ½ inch (1 cm) thick, just like the butter sheet.

Remove the baking paper from the butter and place it on the dough. Fold in the corners / edges of the dough and "seal" in the butter. Roll out into a large rectangle about ½ inch (1 cm) thick. Triple-fold it as in the pictures on page 131. Wrap the dough in plastic wrap and let it rest on the counter for 10 minutes.

Roll out the dough once more and triple-fold it. Wrap the dough in plastic wrap and place in the refrigerator. Rest for about 45 minutes.

Take the dough out, flour it, roll it out once more, and triple-fold it again. Wrap in plastic and place in the refrigerator. Rest for about 45 minutes.

Take the dough out again, flour it, and roll it out one last time. It should be a large oblong rectangle, about ½ inch (1 cm) thick.

Cut off the outer edges of the dough so that you get a nice even rectangle.

1

2

3

Cut out squares about 4 × 4 inches (10 × 10 cm) in size or about 3 ½–4 ounces (100–115 g) in weight.

Now cut out a smaller square inside the first square, about ½ inch (1 cm) in from the edge. Fold one corner of the square toward the other corner diagonally (picture 1). Score straight through the dough (pictures 2 and 3). Fold the square up so that it's flat (picture 4). Take one of the two corners that are open and pull it through the other open corner (pictures 5 and 6). Take both corners and unfold the pastry (see picture of the finished bun on page 148).

Space out evenly on a sheet of baking paper in a deep sheet pan with high edges.

Cover the entire tray / mold with plastic wrap and place low down in the refrigerator until the next day. If the sheet pan doesn't fit in the refrigerator, you can place the Wiener buns closer together in a suitable mold. The next day (when the Wiener buns are cold and hard) it's easier to take them out one by one and space them out evenly on sheet pans. (If you want to bake the Wiener buns the same day, you don't need to wrap them in plastic or place them in the refrigerator. Just let them proof at room temperature.)

Remove the plastic wrap and place the trays in the oven with the light on, but with no heat. Place a small bowl of hot water inside.

Leave to proof for 2–4 hours. They should become significantly larger and fluffier.

Remove the sheet pans and preheat your oven for 1 hour at 480°F (225°C), using the top and bottom elements.

When the oven is hot, pipe a dollop of vanilla cream into the center of each Wiener bun. Bake one sheet at a time in the center of the oven for about 15, until the buns turn golden brown.

Take out and allow to cool. Repeat with the next sheet. Let the buns cool completely before garnishing with icing and fresh berries, if desired. Feel free to sift over some icing sugar.

4

5

6

Stale bread & other tasty recipes

It's sad to have to throw away food, for several reasons. Here are some tips on how you can "reuse" bread that has become old and dry. If you want to make toasted sandwiches or bruschetta, you can use slightly older bread as it will still need to be dried out and toasted in the oven. Livening up a soup by throwing in some bread croutons fried in olive oil also works any day of the week.

A list of how to use bread in other recipes would be long enough to fill another book. Here are a few to start with.

Breadcrumbs

You can make breadcrumbs from any old bread, light or coarse. They'll be tasty regardless. They're absolutely fantastic for meatballs, breaded fish, or similar. You can use the residual heat in the oven after using it to bake bread, for example.

Set the oven to 210°F (100°C).

Slice the stale bread and cut into small chunks. Place the chunks on a sheet pan and put in the lower part of the oven. Let the bread dry out for about 1 hour. Turn off the oven and place a ladle or similar between the oven door and the oven so that the oven door is left slightly ajar while the bread dries out in the residual heat. The bread needs to be completely dry to be pulverized, so if you think it's not quite done, it probably isn't.

If you have a powerful food processor, this is the easiest option. Otherwise, you can put the chunks of bread in double plastic bags and pound or roll them into breadcrumbs. Store in an airtight jar when cool.

Croutons

Homemade croutons for a salad, stew, or soup are really delicious. Light bread and slightly coarse bread work well, although light croutons are more classic. If you have leftover bread that's going stale, croutons are a great idea so you don't waste it.

Set the oven to 350°F (175°C) fan.

Cut your old bread into small chunks and place in a large bowl. Pour over olive oil, salt flakes, a little black pepper, chopped parsley, and a crushed clove of garlic. Massage everything in with your hands.

Pour the chunks onto a sheet pan lined with baking paper and place in a fan-assisted oven at 350°F (175°C) for about 10 minutes. The croutons are ready when they're golden. Remove and serve immediately or store in the dark in an airtight jar.

Tip: You can even freeze old sliced bread to make croutons later on.

Bun crusts

It feels like bun crusts are something that belong to the older generation, mainly because they're the ones who buy them from me. I don't think people appreciate how good bun crusts are, and maybe it doesn't matter all that much ... It can be our little secret. Bun crusts are made from old, leftover buns.

Set the oven to 210°F (100°C).

Cut the old buns into ½-inch (1 cm) thick slices, place them on a sheet pan lined with baking paper, and place in the lower part of the oven. Let the buns dry out for about 1 hour.

Turn the slices halfway through the baking time, as the tops of the buns often dry out faster. Turn off the oven and place a ladle or similar between the oven door and the oven so that the oven door is left slightly ajar while the bread dries out in the residual heat.

Leave to cool and then store in an airtight jar. Bun crusts usually last a few weeks, provided your tummy doesn't get to them first.

Toasted hazelnut granola

If you bake regularly, you have almost all the ingredients at home that you need to throw together a fantastically delicious granola. If you want to make the granola a little extra special, you can buy some dried fruit and add it after toasting.

Weight		Ingredients
14 oz.	(400 g)	oatmeal
7 oz.	(200 g)	hazelnuts
3 ½ oz.	(100 g)	sunflower seeds
1 ¾ oz.	(50 g)	sesame seeds
1 ¾ oz.	(50 g)	flax seeds
8 ½ oz.	(240 g)	honey
5 ⅔ oz.	(160 g)	mild cooking oil, e. g. rapeseed oil
¼ oz.	(8 g)	salt
¼ oz.	(8 g)	cinnamon
4 g		cardamom
4 g		ginger
		+ raisins, cranberries, dried papaya (or whatever you like)

Set the oven to 350°F (175°C).

Mix the oil, honey, salt, and spices and bring to a boil in a saucepan on the stove. Remove the saucepan from the stove and let it cool.

Spread all the other ingredients (except the fruit) on a sheet pan lined with baking paper. Pour over the cooled oil mixture and massage into the seed mixture. Spread everything evenly over the sheet pan and then place it in the center of the oven. The granola needs to toast for 20–30 minutes. I usually set a timer for 15 minutes. When the time is up, I mix everything around with a large spoon. I then set a timer for 5 minutes and check every time it rings so that the granola doesn't get too dark. That said, it's good if the granola turns golden and a little toasted in color and flavor.

Tips & Tricks

Generally, my recipes are based on five hours of proofing atroom temperature. This is the time from when you mix the dough until you put it in the refrigerator. Five hours is usually enough to make well-proofed bread, if you bake with a sourdough that's fed according to my instructions.

But keep in mind that it's the temperature that determines how quickly your dough proofs, and therefore it's ultimately the volume of the dough that determines when it's ready. The dough should be considerably larger when you put it in the refrigerator. It should feel airy and almost bouncy, like an inflated balloon, especially if it's a light dough. If it doesn't, you need to let the dough proof for longer. Wait another hour before shaping, or place the dough in the proofing basket and let it sit there for an hour or two before placing it in the refrigerator.

Do I always need to fold the dough four times?

Yes and no. It's recommended to do this when mixing by hand for several reasons.

If you mix the dough using a machine, two folds may be enough, but this is something you can experiment with yourself. The folding acts as a kind of gentle kneading, helps distribute gases, and evens out the temperature in the dough. If you use a machine, some of this comes included in the process. However, from an educational perspective, it's very useful to fold the dough. This lets you physically observe the dough's transformation as it grows bigger, airier, and more beautiful over time. In this way you'll learn to read when the dough is ready and also notice if it's proofing faster or slower.

Coarse Dough

Doughs with a lot of rye or wholemeal flour don't need to be processed in the same way as lighter doughs. This is noticeable in my recipes for shaped breads, for example. They're not folded as many times and no direct shaping or final shape is needed. Really coarse doughs just break down the more you handle them, so it's best to leave them alone. So, when should you (and when should you not) fold or shape a dough? When you can fold without the dough breaking, you fold. The same applies to shaping/final shape.

Mix in all the water right away or hold back?

There are several reasons why I usually wait to mix in the last bit of water when mixing the dough. The first reason is that it makes it easier for the salt to be well-distributed throughout the dough. The second reason is to protect us against weak flour. The third reason is that when mixing wet dough with a lot of water, it's easier to achieve a stronger dough (which will hold its shape more easily during preshape/final shape and baking) if you hold back the remaining water. Without overcomplicating things, it's about giving the gluten the friction it needs to achieve optimal development. For comparison, you can think of it this way... In a super-soft pancake batter, there's zero gluten. There's simply too much liquid for the flour to bind properly into a dough. In a dry dough, the dough becomes hard and strong immediately. You can capitalize on this by gradually increasing the amount of water. The gluten will be stronger to start with, before softening as you add the remaining water. This is instead of trying to force the flour to create gluten in a hopelessly wet batter.

As a general rule, I mix in all the water immediately for doughs with 65-percent hydration. For hydration levels above that, I hold back some water, which I then mix in with the salt, and sometimes even during the first folds. The wetter the dough, the more important this is. Adding the water in stages like this is called *bassinage* in French baking parlance.

Why is my dough so sticky?

Assume that your bread doughs will be sticky and quite loose. Sourdough baking generally uses much more water than in traditional bread recipes. This is the essence of making this "type" of bread. So, it's not necessarily wrong just because it feels strange or unfamiliar. On the contrary, it's entirely normal for things to feel a little weird and strange if you haven't worked with this type of bread dough before. Give it time, and it will feel completely natural.

Winter—the slowest season for sourdough

In winter, it can sometimes feel like the dough is stone dead and nothing is happening. It may therefore be a good idea to use slightly warmer water for both your sourdough and bread dough and also try to find a warmer place to keep the dough bowl between all the steps. This could be above the refrigerator or in a turned-off oven that's been preheated for half a minute or so, just so it starts to get going a little. Leave the oven light on, just to heat it up slightly.

Scoring bread

By scoring the bread, we allow it to expand and crack open nicely and become as big as it wants. If we don't score the bread, it will often turn out smaller and/or uneven and denser in texture on the inside. I recommend using a razor blade or a paring knife with replaceable blades. Bread dough is sticky so you need something thin and sharp to make fine scores.

Baking paper or not?

Using baking paper is much easier than not using it. I usually use baking paper when baking bread on a baking steel as it's easier to slide a whole sheet of baking paper into the oven than each bread one by one. When it comes to baking bread in a pot, although I never use baking paper myself, I recommend you do so when you start out baking. This will make it easier to place the bread in the hot pot and you'll avoid the bread sticking, which it sometimes has a tendency to do. Some molds are completely useless and require baking paper, while others have a nonstick coating that works better. Oiling baking pans with a neutral oil can help the bread to release better.

Baking

I recommend baking most breads in a pot at 450°F (230°C), using the top and bottom elements for 20 minutes with the lid on and 20 minutes with the lid off. This is the easiest way to get a good and even result, without a burnt bottom. So follow these instructions until you get the hang of your breads and your oven.

You can, of course, bake at a higher or lower temperature and also adjust the baking time. In simple terms, the longer you bake, the more you dry out the bread. The outside, or crust, dries first. This means that if you bake for a long time, you'll get a thicker, more robust crust. This also usually means you get a darker baked bread, but you can counter this by baking at a slightly lower temperature if you prefer a thick crust. Conversely, bake for a slightly shorter time if you want a nice, thin crust. But remember you'll need to bake at a slightly higher temperature so that the whole bread has time to bake. You can control this yourself... It's trial and error. The hardest thing about baking hot and fast is that the underside often burns, so it takes some practice before you get exactly the result you want.

To complicate things further, different breads bake at different speeds. As a general rule, light breads bake quicker, as they are often airier than coarse breads. Lastly, all breads will also bake differently depending on how well-proofed they are. If well-proofed, they bake quickly, as they contain a lot of air/gas. If they're not as well-proofed, they'll take more time.

Pot, baking steel, or sheet pan?

When I bake "normal-sized" bread at home, I always use a cast iron pan that can withstand the heat of the oven. I've tried a lot of different ways but always come back to the pot. It works best for me.

The positive thing about baking in a pot is that it mimics the environment of a bakery oven, albeit on a smaller scale. A bakery oven has a relatively low oven chamber, which ensures that the heat is evenly distributed around the bread. A bakery oven also has a steam function, which means you can add steam with the simple push of a button.

When you bake bread in a pot, you bake the bread in a tighter oven cavity. The heat will be very even around the entire bread because you've preheated the entire pot properly before you put the bread in. Bread gives off a lot of water—which becomes steam—when baking. When you bake in a pot, this steam is retained and envelops the bread for the first twenty minutes. This prevents the crust from drying out and hardening too quickly, giving the bread the opportunity to expand.

The downside to baking in a pot is that you can only bake bread of a certain size and only bake one loaf at a time.

The next best option is, I think, to bake on a baking steel, or pizza steel. You can then bake two breads at once, which saves time. This also works great for rolls, pizzas, and other slightly larger breads. A baking steel is a roughly ¼-inch (6–8 mm) thick sheet that is heated up in the same way as a pot. When baking, this heat is sent up into the bread and allows the bread to expand. To create steam, place an oven-safe dish (which you also preheat) at the bottom of the oven and pour boiling water into it when you place the bread in. I usually heat water in a coffee cup in the microwave and pour it into the dish when it's time. A coffee cup usually holds ½–1 cup (100–200 ml) of water, which is usually enough. I recommend you remove the water dish halfway through the baking time, but usually all the water has evaporated by this point, so I usually just leave the dish in place, especially if I'm going to bake more bread.

The worst way to bake bread is to use a sheet pan. It's still possible to make some kind of edible bread if you don't have either a pot or a baking steel, so give it a try if you want. If so, preheat a sheet pan onto which you can slide the bread using a peel or similar.

I think quite a few of us have baked pizza at home in the oven on a cold sheet pan and then wondered why the pizza is doughy and unbaked on the bottom and especially in the middle. That's because bread needs to be heated from all sides. A thin sheet pan doesn't have time to get hot enough before the pizza cools the sheet. The logic is quite easy to understand when you watch Neapolitan pizza bakers fire up their stone ovens and bake pizzas at nearly 950°F (500°C). Compare that to trying to bake on a room-temperature sheet pan.

Bread in molds

Baking bread in a mold is quite nice as you can skip several steps. What can be a bit tricky is that you're not as in touch with the dough because it gets put in a mold quite early on and is left to its own devices to proof. What I find most difficult when it comes to baking in a mold is judging the level of proofing and knowing when the dough is ready. That's why I'm extra careful to look closely at how big the bread has become in the mold before I bake it, so that I have that as a reference for the next time I make the same recipe.

It's also a bit tricky to know if the breads are ready in the oven when you can only see the top, so I have a habit of always taking the temperature of my breads with a probe thermometer. I want the bread to have an internal temperature of 210°F (100°C) before I take it out of the oven.

Generally, my mold-based recipes are on the coarser side. These doughs are quite difficult to mix by hand, so having a machine makes it easier. For these doughs, I find it extra important to hold back some water, to both distribute the salt evenly and get more of a feel for the dough. Sometimes the dough becomes rock hard and you may need to add a little more water. Sometimes the flour absorbs less water than usual and then you don't need to add the last bit of water.

SVEBA DAHLEN

Rolls

Bread rolls are one of the easiest, most forgiving, and perhaps tastiest things to make when you're starting out. You can choose almost any recipe, such as a recipe with fruit and nuts, and when it's time to preshape, you put the entire batch of dough in the refrigerator until the next day instead. What really distinguishes a bread dough and a roll dough is how you choose to shape the breads.

Storing bread

Bread is a perishable product and will gradually dry out if you don't eat it up. The bread becomes dry because the moisture wants to leave the bread. Most people have probably baked a sponge cake that they forgot to put plastic wrap around before going to bed and the next day it was almost inedible.

As I see it, you really have two choices when it comes to storing bread. One is in a plastic bag, which traps the moisture best and results in a soft and chewy crust. The other option is to store it in a cloth bag or wrap it in a linen towel or kitchen towel, which will preserve the crust of the bread. This will protect the bread from drying out to some extent but it will still dry out faster than if stored in plastic.

Sourdough bread with its slightly thicker crust has the ability to encapsulate moisture better than "regular" bread and it's mainly the end slice that becomes dry. I believe that bread that is allowed to breathe develops flavor and gets better over time, which is why I prefer to store the bread in a cloth bag, but that's just my personal opinion. Although my wife prefers to put the bread in a plastic bag.

Slicing the bread, wrapping it in plastic wrap, and putting it in the freezer to then thaw in the toaster when you need it is also a great option for always having good toast.

How long can bread dough stay in the refrigerator?

Bread dough can usually be kept in the refrigerator for one to two days before baking. Sometimes you can get away with three days, but usually the bread will be a little flatter and more sour. I believe that bread is best when baked after a night's rest in the refrigerator, so that's how I do it both at home and in the bakery. This affects both the taste and the shape of the final bread.

When it comes to doughs for rolls or pizza, however, I think you can push the boundaries a bit and keep them an extra day or two in the refrigerator.

Baking the same day—pros and cons

Does the dough need to be put in the refrigerator overnight for it to be good? Yes and no. This is mainly about making sure the dough is fully proofed and develops flavor. For more "common" sourdough bread that proofs in a proofing basket, it's also easier to bake bread that has been in the refrigerator because the dough has tightened up a bit in the cold, making it easier for you to score the bread and achieve a smoother and finer result on the final loaf. If you want, or need, to bake the same day you make the dough, that's perfectly fine, but try to place the dough in the refrigerator for a few hours before baking. You'll get a milder bread because the lactic acid bacteria haven't had as long in the refrigerator to proof the bread.

Some breads in the book are mixed and baked on the same day, but that's usually for a reason, such as to ensure the best taste or shape of the final bread. That said, you *can* bake all the breads on the same day or let them rest in the refrigerator until the next day.

Internal temperature

If you have a probe thermometer, light breads are ready when the internal temperature is 205°F (96°C) or above, and really coarse breads should reach an internal temperature of 210°F (100°C).

Wheat or rye sourdough?

I work almost exclusively with a wheat sourdough because I find it easiest to control the flavor. The main difference between a wheat sourdough and, for example, a rye sourdough is that they flavor the final bread in different ways. It's perfectly fine to "convert" your wheat sourdough into a rye sourdough and vice versa if, for example, you're going to bake a rye bread and want to make the bread exclusively with rye. You then feed your wheat sourdough solely with rye for a while and eventually the majority of its content will be rye. It's as simple as it sounds. The sourdough wants nutrition and the nutrition is found in the sugar in the starch in the flour, regardless of whether that sugar comes from wheat or rye flour. I use a dash of rye in my wheat sourdough because rye flour is rich in microorganisms.

Sourdough discard

Sourdough discard can be used for quite a lot if you think it's a shame to throw it away. Pancake and waffle batter, cookie batter, biscuits, and so on. You can easily find recipes by googling "sourdough discard recipes". These are recipes where you don't necessarily need proofing. Old sourdough discard that's left to sit and ferment in the refrigerator doesn't proof very well. However, it can be used as a flavoring and perhaps primarily as a way to reuse the flour. If you want to use old sourdough, you can make sure that every time you scrape it out to feed your sourdough, you scrape it out into another jar that you store in the refrigerator, instead of throwing it away.

Salt

To be completely honest, it doesn't really matter what salt you use in your bread dough. I've tried regular salt, with and without iodine, salt flakes, rock salt, sea salt, and so on. I always work with unrefined fine sea salt in the bakery because I want to keep my breads as natural as possible, but just because I do it doesn't mean you have to. It is said that iodine inhibits proofing, but the small amount found in iodized salt has no noticeable effect.

However, salt itself inhibits proofing and that's why I wait to mix it into the dough. If you are short on time, you can mix in the salt immediately, but then you'll need to add an hour or two to the proofing time to get the same volume of dough. Alternatively, proof at a slightly higher temperature. However, I rarely do it that way, because I find it easier to be consistent in my approach and I feel that I don't get as good results when I mix in the salt directly. Then there are always exceptions. For me it's usually due to slightly different doughs, such as extremely coarse breads that don't need to be shaped in the same way as regular breads. All bakers do things differently because we all develop ways that work best for us, which you'll see yourself if you read different books or recipes.

Regarding the amount of salt in bread dough, it's a matter of taste. A rule of thumb is that 2 percent salt in relation to the weight of flour is almost always sufficient. I consider 3 percent salt to be the maximum and I never go above that.

If I were to try to give a kind of scale, all my "regular" breads usually contain exactly 2 percent salt. Baguettes, ciabatta, or lighter breads that are supposed to be a little more flavorful often contain around 2.5 percent salt. My porridge breads also contain 2.5 percent salt, but that's mainly because the baking math for these breads is a bit incorrect in that they add so much by way of groats that also needs to be salted. Heartier breads like focaccia, pizza, and the like are usually good with 2.75 percent and even up to 3 percent if you're very fond of salt.

Amount of salt in doughs with 28 ¼ ounces (800 g) of flour. Here I have only stated the value in grams, as ounce measures are slightly less accurate:

2 % = 16 g of salt
2.25 % = 18 g of salt
2.5 % = 20 g of salt
2.75 % = 22 g of salt
3 % = 24 g of salt

When it comes to salt in sweet breads, I use it sparingly. Salt is great in sweet things to bring out flavors, but without tasting salty. For these recipes, I think 1–1.5 percent is a good rule of thumb.

Tip: Cultivated grains and flours, made from einkorn, emmer, and rye for example, are in principle sold exclusively by artisanal mills. Many artisanal mills have good webshops where you can easily click and buy the flour you want.

Sugar

I usually use two types of sugar—regular white granulated sugar and raw cane sugar.
Most people are familiar with granulated sugar. It's the sweetest, which I prefer for most sweet doughs. Raw cane sugar, which is a little darker and often a little coarser, has a broader flavor profile and is good to use when you want more depth of flavor than just sweet. That's why I often use this for butter fillings and the like. But it really is a matter of taste and preference. Both work just as well in all recipes.

Spices

Adding spices to bread is both delicious and exciting. However, I find that spices can easily dominate the flavor palette, so season carefully. In bread that needs to be very flavorful, such as sourdough bread, I usually add 1 percent spice in relation to the weight of the flour. In other breads where I don't want the spice to be as dominant, 0.25–0.5 percent is usually a good guideline.

Amount of spice in doughs with 28 ¼ ounces (800 g) of flour. Again, here I have only stated the value in grams, as ounce measures are slightly less accurate:
1 % = 8 g of spices
0.75 % = 6 g of spices
0.5 % = 4 g of spices
0.25 % = 2 g of spices

You can see this in my recipes, but it can be a good idea to keep this cheat sheet to hand if you want to experiment with your own recipes. Remember that this is a recommendation rather than a rule.

It's always better to use whole spices that you mortar or mix yourself than pre-ground spices, which quickly lose their flavor.

Tip: My mom taught me that if you don't have a mortar, you can use a rolling pin and crush them against a cutting board.

Flour & Milling

As many of you probably know, our four grains are wheat, barley, oats, and rye. Thanks to increased interest, many variations of these are now available, and the term cultured grain is something that is heard a lot nowadays. The oldest varieties are einkorn and emmer, which are grass-related wheat varieties. They're closely followed by spelt and various varieties of common wheat.

Plant evolution has occurred naturally over thousands of years. As I understand it, all of the above varieties have been created through naturally occurring cross-pollination with wild grasses. In modern times, and especially over the last 50 years, we have bred, or hybridized, an incredible number of wheat varieties. It's said that there are now nearly 25,000 different varieties. This is for two reasons—to get better yields and to improve the baking properties of the flour. Better baking properties often mean a stronger flour, with a gluten that produces large, airy loaves.

Today, we've reintroduced and begun growing several older crops, so-called cultured grains, something that I and many other bakers are happy about as it creates diversity and variation in flavor. Variety is the spice of life, as they say.

Wheat flour is the flour I use the most. Whether you bake hundreds of loaves in a day like I do at the bakery, or make two loaves at home in your kitchen, it's nice to use a flour you can rely on. A flour that delivers. Sourdough baking is sensitive enough as it is, so using a reliable flour is nice. That's why I mostly used to use bread flour as my base flour. I mainly use various older varieties of wholemeal flours and cultured grains as a flavoring, except when I deliberately bake very coarse breads, or when I'm looking to try a different type of bread. This is also my unwavering recommendation to anyone starting out with baking sourdough bread. Use a strong flour when you're learning... It's complicated enough as it is. Once you've got the hang of the basics, you can start to explore the spectrum of flours and discover new flavors.

I need to generalize a bit to try and explain my reasoning. When we talk about different wheat flours, *strong* and *weak* flours are often mentioned. Strong flour means that the gluten quality is good, binds a lot of water, and creates a nice and strong gluten network—that's what holds the dough and gas together in the bread. A strong wheat flour produces high and airy breads. To create a reliable baking flour, the solution is often to mix the two different varieties until you get a sufficiently good and high-quality flour composition.

In older sifted types of wheat flour, cultivated varieties such as spelt and common wheat, gluten quality is rarely checked in the same way. Sometimes you end up with a rather weak flour and sometimes the flour turns out to be great and makes super delicious bread. As a baker, you need to be aware of these when using these varieties. It's something that I find frustrating at times, but also rewarding in equal measure. Cultured grains, with their slightly weaker gluten and slightly different taste, create very creamy breads.

To generalize further. A strong flour doesn't stick as much and holds its shape better during the various stages, such as when the dough is being divided into several smaller balls.

A weaker flour is more sticky and liquid-like when you work with the dough. This is something you'll notice yourself if you try baking with different types of flour. There are ways to correct this, and the simplest is to follow the logic that a weak flour doesn't absorb as much liquid. That's why I always start with less water when baking with sifted cultured grains and gradually add more water if I feel the dough can handle it. This is something that can be difficult to get the hang of at first, but it will come with experience.

Einkorn

Einkorn, the true ancient grain, began to be cultivated more than 10,000 years ago in the Middle East. It contains only one kernel in each spikelet, hence the name, which means "single kernel". Einkorn has a high nutritional content, but a weak gluten. The flour has a yellowish tone as it contains carotenoids, an antioxidant. It's very nice, and a personal favorite when it comes to taste. Einkorn is usually milled as a wholemeal flour, but it's also available as a sifted flour.

Emmer

Emmer began to be cultivated around 8,000 years ago. It is a cross between einkorn and wild grass. This flour is strong in its gluten, very tasty, and quite reminiscent of einkorn in terms of baking properties. Emmer is sometimes also referred to as white or black, depending on whether it's sown in spring or autumn. Emmer is usually milled as a wholemeal flour.

Durum

Durum wheat is related to emmer and is a hard yellowish wheat that is often used for pasta. It's fun to mix in a little durum wheat into different breads for color, flavor, and a little more crunch. Usually durum flour, or durum wheat flour, is a sifted flour, but it can be found as wholemeal flour.

Spelt

Spelt is around 5,000 years old. Just like einkorn and emmer, the kernels are embedded in a thick shell that protects them from air pollution and means it needs to be shelled before it can be milled. Something unique about spelt is that much of the nutrition is in the endosperm, which means that sifted spelt flour is healthier than sifted wheat flour, for example. Spelt flour can be found as both sifted and wholemeal flour. You can use wholemeal flour just like graham flour, for example. Sifted spelt is generally quite weak and loose. It can be a little harder to get the dough to hold together well, but it's delicious!

Rye

Rye has been grown and eaten for a long time in the Nordic countries because it's easier to grow in their slightly colder climate. Rye is healthy, rich in dietary fiber, tastes great, and fills you up for a long time. Rye has a slightly stronger flavor than many other grains, while also having a subtle sweetness. That all adds up to make rye one of the most exciting types of flour to use as a flavoring in bread. I prefer to bake a dough with a lot of rye so that it has a relatively dark crust, as that brings out even more flavors. Rye has a different gluten composition than wheat, and a dough with a lot of rye will always be quite sticky. Rye comes in several forms. Rye flour almost always means wholemeal rye flour and is often available in both fine-milled and coarse-milled varieties.

Sifted rye blend flour

Traditional sifted rye is a light flour blend containing 40 percent sifted rye and 60 percent wheat flour.

Unblended sifted rye flour

As the name suggests, this is only sifted rye flour. So, 100 percent sifted rye flour. It's good flavoring flour to use to get a slightly milder rye flavor in the bread.

Landrace rye flour

An older rye variety that got its name from landrace cultivation, which involved burning forests to make room for sowing grain. Landrace flour is slightly more nutritious than traditional rye and is perceived as having a slightly milder taste, at least by me. Otherwise, I use it just like regular rye.

Bread flour

Wheat flour is the most commonly used flour in many places around the globe. Bread flour is a highly sifted wheat flour that is well suited for baking bread. It maintains a high gluten quality that creates nice, easy-to-work doughs that usually rise nicely in the oven.

Heritage wheat flour

Older varieties of wheat flour are known as heritage grains. I and many other bakers use these heritage varieties because they taste good and often have relatively good baking properties. These varieties are often available as both sifted flours and wholemeal flours. I use the wholemeal flours in the same way as graham flour. The sifted flours I use instead of bread flour, or I replace half or part of it to get a slightly different taste and character in the final bread. If you can get hold of it, I would recommend trying Öland wheat flour, which is becoming increasingly available in many places around the world.

Graham flour

Wholemeal wheat flour. Compared to refined flour, wholemeal wheat flour is made from grinding the entire grain, which makes it more nutritious and healthier.

Milling

There are many different flours and flour types. These stem from the different varieties as well as from how the flour is milled. There are essentially two different types—sifted flour and wholemeal flour. Flour is milled from whole grains. A grain consists of endosperm, bran (shell), and germ. Bran and germ become larger pieces when the flour is milled, while the endosperm is pulverized. This makes it relatively easy to sift out the endosperm, which gives us fine white flour. Wholemeal flour, as the name suggests, means that the whole (entire) grain has been milled and that everything ends up in the bag, so to speak. Generally, most of the nutrients are found in the bran and germ, which means that wholemeal bread is more or less always healthier than lighter bread.

Sifted flour produces white breads. Wholemeal flour produces dark breads. A mixture of the two flours produces different shades of bread, from lighter to darker.

A fine-mesh cloth is used to sift the flour. In a mill, there are cloths of varying fineness through which the flour is passed to sift out all the shell parts. What remains at the bottom will be a fine, light flour. Depending on how finely the flour is sifted, it will be of varying lightness. A typical old-fashioned flour is not sifted as finely (because it wasn't previously possible), so that's why it's called what it is.

There is also a difference between wholemeal flours, to complicate things further. Flour is mostly commonly *roller milled*, which means that the grains are pressed between two steel rollers or cylinders. The different parts are separated. The shell goes in one direction and the endosperm goes in another, where it is then sifted. The parts are then mixed together again to create a wholemeal flour.

Artisanal mills often use an older method of milling, known as *stone-ground*. The whole grains are milled between two rotating stone discs into a finished wholemeal flour. Sometimes they also make sifted flour in the stone mill. Here, the flour is sifted after milling, resulting in a slightly darker, slightly more flavorful sifted flour.

Another term you might stumble across is *vortex-milled* flour. This means that the flour is milled against a stone in a stream of air into an incredibly fine-milled wholemeal flour. This takes place in a so-called vortex mill. Vortex-milled wholemeal flour generally gives breads with a slightly better volume than other wholemeal flours.

In summary, it can be said that wholemeal flour is the healthiest flour, and especially rye, because of its nutritional content. It's worth mentioning here that cultured grains are also said to have a higher nutritional content than modern wheat varieties, as well as a gluten composition that is supposed to be more easily digestible for our stomachs. This means that sifted cultured grains are preferable to modern wheat flours if you're primarily looking for better nutritional content.

The easiest flour to bake with, however, is the flour that sticks the least and holds its shape the best, and the flour that produces the highest and airiest bread, which is a strong modern-milled sifted wheat flour.

As you may have noticed, there are two fairly clear parameters to bear in mind here. What is important to you when baking bread? I want my breads to be airy and hold their shape well. At the same time, I want them to be healthy and nutritious. A natural choice for me then is to mix different flours.

The Bakery

At three o'clock on a Saturday morning, the smell of freshly baked bread and buns begins to waft through the cottages in the residential area of Kullavik where I run my bakery, *Surdegsgott—Kullavik's little artisan bakery.* My bakery has been up and running for almost three years and is housed in the garage on our property. I converted it into a bakery to accommodate a large oven so I could bake more bread and to devote more time to my hobby—sourdough baking. This so-called hobby has, as you may have guessed, gotten a little out of hand. It's now my job.

The smell of freshly baked bread, a bakery, is an aroma and a romantic feeling that many can relate to. It's mainly people from the older generation who notice this: "Oh, this smell is so wonderful, I remember when my dad came home with freshly baked bread from the local bakery when I was little." However, children's reactions are always the funniest. Eyes as big as ping-pong balls trying to scan everything and find what looks tastiest. Their tongues almost hang out of their mouths: "Look at how much bread there is! Daddy, I want buns!" Then, when I hand over the brown paper bag with the freshly baked bread, they start squeezing and exploring: "It's still warm, Mom, touch it!"

The fascination with freshly baked warm bread is almost universal… Everyone reacts the same way. It evokes joy.

SVEBA DAHLEN
SURDEGSGOTT

Directory

Sourdough for All

Text by Kenny Jakobsson

Copy editing of the English edition by GLOBALscandinavia for booklab GmbH, Munich

Photography by Stefan Wettainen

Cover and layout by gestalten

Production management by Martin Bretschneider

Typefaces: *Superior Title* by Jeremy Mickel and *Utopia Std* by Robert Slimbach

Printed by Printer Trento s. r. l., Trento
Made in Italy

Published by gestalten, Berlin 2025
ISBN 978-3-96704-181-1

1st printing, 2025

The Swedish original edition *Surdegsbröd för alla* was published by Bokförlaget Polaris

English edition published in agreement with Politiken Literary Agency and Bennet Agency

For more information, and to order books, please visit www.gestalten.com.

Die Gestalten Verlag GmbH & Co. KG
Mariannenstrasse 9–10
10999 Berlin, Germany
hello@gestalten.com

Bibliographic information published by the Deutsche Nationalbibliothek.
The Deutsche Nationalbibliothek lists this publication in the Deutsche Nationalbibliografie; detailed bibliographic data are available online at www.dnb.de.

This book was printed on paper certified according to the standards of the FSC®.